THE BEDFORD SERIES IN HIST

Lenin and the Making of the Soviet State

A Brief History with Documents

Jeffrey Brooks

The Johns Hopkins University

Georgiy Chernyavskiy

Ukrainian Academy of Culture, Professor Emeritus

BEDFORD/ST. MARTIN'S   Boston ♦ New York

For Bedford/St. Martin's

Publisher for History: Mary V. Dougherty
Executive Editor for History: Katherine Meisenheimer
Director of Development for History: Jane Knetzger
Developmental Editor: Melissa Mashburn
Senior Production Supervisor: Dennis J. Conroy
Production Associate: Matthew P. Hayes
Senior Marketing Manager: Jenna Bookin Barry
Project Management: Books By Design, Inc.
Text Design: Claire Seng-Niemoeller
Indexing: Books By Design, Inc.
Cover Design: Billy Boardman
Cover Art: Lenin at the Second Conference of the Communist International, July–August 1920. Prints and Photographs Division, Library of Congress, LC-USZ62-64912.
Composition: Stratford Publishing Services, Inc.
Printing and Binding: RR Donnelley & Sons Company

President: Joan E. Feinberg
Editorial Director: Denise B. Wydra
Director of Marketing: Karen Melton Soeltz
Director of Editing, Design, and Production: Marcia Cohen
Manager, Publishing Services: Emily Berleth

Library of Congress Control Number: 2006923857

Manufactured in the United States of America.

2   1   0   9   8   7
f   e   d   c   b   a

For information, write: Bedford/St. Martin's, 75 Arlington Street, Boston, MA 02116
(617-399-4000)

ISBN-10: 0-312-41266-5 (paperback)
        0-312-1-4039-7158-7 (hardcover)
ISBN-13: 978-0-312-41266-1

Acknowledgments

Documents 33, 45, 50, 54, 55: From *The Unknown Lenin: From the Secret Archive*, edited by Richard Pipes (New Haven, Conn.: Yale University Press). Copyright © 1996 by Yale University.

Document 56: From *Lenin's Will: Falsified and Forbidden. From the Secret Archives of the Former Soviet Union*, by Yuri Buranov (Amherst, N.Y.: Prometheus Books). Copyright © 1994 by Yuri Buranov. Reprinted with permission.

Foreword

The Bedford Series in History and Culture is designed so that readers can study the past as historians do.

The historian's first task is finding the evidence. Documents, letters, memoirs, interviews, pictures, movies, novels, or poems can provide facts and clues. Then the historian questions and compares the sources. There is more to do than in a courtroom, for hearsay evidence is welcome, and the historian is usually looking for answers beyond act and motive. Different views of an event may be as important as a single verdict. How a story is told may yield as much information as what it says.

Along the way the historian seeks help from other historians and perhaps from specialists in other disciplines. Finally, it is time to write, to decide on an interpretation and how to arrange the evidence for readers.

Each book in this series contains an important historical document or group of documents, each document a witness from the past and open to interpretation in different ways. The documents are combined with some element of historical narrative—an introduction or a biographical essay, for example—that provides students with an analysis of the primary source material and important background information about the world in which it was produced.

Each book in the series focuses on a specific topic within a specific historical period. Each provides a basis for lively thought and discussion about several aspects of the topic and the historian's role. Each is short enough (and inexpensive enough) to be a reasonable one-week assignment in a college course. Whether as classroom or personal reading, each book in the series provides firsthand experience of the challenge— and fun—of discovering, recreating, and interpreting the past.

Lynn Hunt
David W. Blight
Bonnie G. Smith
Natalie Zemon Davis
Ernest R. May

Preface

V. I. Lenin is one of the few modern political leaders who changed the course of history and helped bring something unique into the world. Like Mussolini and Hitler, Lenin invented a new political system, established new forms of economic relations, and set in place a new social order. Nazism and Italian fascism perished in World War II, but Lenin's Soviet Union lived on, inspiring like-minded leaders elsewhere to create what amounted to one-party states, especially in the third world and among former colonies. At the turn of the twenty-first century, Leninist-type governments still ruled China, Vietnam, North Korea, and Cuba, as well as parts of Africa and the Middle East.

As the founder of the Soviet state and a key player in the development of its policies, Lenin shaped Russian history. The Soviet Union was the fulfillment of Lenin's vision, but it was also the outgrowth of a particular historical situation and of the struggles between his supporters and his opponents. This text seeks to document Lenin's ideas, his plans for Russia, and the policies he instituted by allowing Lenin to reveal himself through his own words. Our selection of documents is designed to provide readers with a better understanding of Lenin's role in the Soviet state's development.

This book should prove helpful to students of world history, European and Russian history, political science, and international relations. The introductory essay describes Russia in the late nineteenth and early twentieth centuries and provides an overview of Lenin's life, allowing students to follow Lenin's evolution from an angry dissident student to an adept political organizer and theoretician. The introduction concludes with a discussion of Lenin's last years that raises the question of whether the ailing leader actually tried to shape the country's future and pick his successor or simply wallowed in indecision, unable to imagine ceding control of the country to any of his colleagues.

Part Two of the text is divided into four chapters that focus on the formation of Lenin's main ideas and their practical fulfillment during the Russian Revolution, the ensuing Civil War, popular unrest and the development of the New Economic Policy, and Lenin's conflicts with Bolshevik Party leaders over the direction of the party during his protracted final illness. The documents include key theoretical works as well as appeals to the populace and party activists, such as his "Open Letter to the Delegates of the All-Russian Congress of Peasants' Deputies" from May 1917 (Document 9) and his "Speech to Propagandists on Their Way to the Provinces" from February 1918 (Document 17). A selection of pragmatic statements and secret policy directives reveals a ruthless, authoritarian side of Lenin that he did not wish to make public. To show how he secretly shaped policy, we include his pronouncement on the "Organization of Food Detachments" from June 1918 (Document 35), which set in motion the forcible seizure of peasants' surpluses, as well as his recently revealed "strictly secret" letter to Molotov for members of the Central Committee detailing his plans for a campaign against the Orthodox Church in March 1922 (Document 54).

Each chapter begins with a brief introduction. The documents are accompanied by headnotes and explanatory gloss notes. At the end of the text, additional pedagogical elements include a chronology of Lenin's life, a set of questions for consideration and further discussion, and a bibliographical guide to further readings. Photographs of Lenin and his inner circle are provided in the text's introduction.

A NOTE ABOUT THE TEXT

The collapse of the Soviet Union and the opening of Soviet archives have made it possible to document Lenin's role in the inner workings of the Bolshevik dictatorship more fully than was possible in the past. Among the fine collections of documents that have been translated into English are *The Unknown Lenin: From the Secret Archive*, edited by Richard Pipes (New Haven and London: Yale University Press, 1996), and *Lenin's Will: Falsified and Forbidden. From the Secret Archives of the Former Soviet Union* by Yuri Buranov (Amherst, N.Y.: Prometheus Books, 1994). We thank the authors and publishers of these volumes for permission to include selected documents from these works.

We have used the Library of Congress system of transliteration of Russian names, but have kept the accepted English usage of familiar names such as that of Trotsky. Until February 1918, Russians used the Julian calendar, which was 12 days behind the Gregorian calendar in the nineteenth century and 13 days behind the Gregorian in the twentieth century. As a result, the February Revolution actually took place in March according to contemporary dating. New-style dates are given in parentheses when appropriate.

ACKNOWLEDGMENTS

We are particularly grateful to Melissa Mashburn, our developmental editor. We also warmly thank Mary Dougherty, executive editor; Jane Knetzger, director of development; and Shannon Hunt, associate editor at Bedford/St. Martin's, and Nancy Benjamin at Books By Design. We are also grateful to our reviewers. They include Dmitry Shlapentokh, Indiana University–South Bend; John Bushnell, Northwestern University; Kenneth Moss, The Johns Hopkins University; Peter Kenez, University of California, Santa Cruz; John Thomas Sanders, United States Naval Academy; Elizabeth Jane Dennison, University of Alaska–Anchorage; Steven G. Marks, Clemson University; and a reviewer who wished to remain anonymous, whom we also thank. Their comments were to the point and helped focus and improve the text. Any shortcomings that remain, however, are the responsibility of the authors alone. Finally, Jeff Brooks thanks his wife, Karen, and Georgiy Chernyavskiy thanks his dear friend, Larisa Dubova.

Jeffrey Brooks
Georgiy Chernyavskiy

Contents

Foreword   iii

Preface   v

PART ONE
Introduction: V. I. Lenin's Life and Legacy   **1**

V. I. Lenin and the Founding of the Soviet State   1

The Russia of Lenin's Youth   3

Lenin as Revolutionary   7

World War I and the Russian Revolution   12

Bolshevik Rule and the New Soviet State   17

War Communism: Ideology or Pragmatism?   20

Lenin's Last Active Years: The New Economic Policy and
Other Innovations   22

Lenin's Decline   25

Lenin's Legacy   29

PART TWO
The Documents   **35**

**1. Lenin and the Bolshevik Seizure of Power,
   1900–1917**   **37**

Lenin as a Theorist of Revolution   **38**

1. From *The Urgent Tasks of Our Movement*, December
   1900   38

2. From *What Is to Be Done?* 1902   39

3. From *The Party Organization and Party Literature,*
    November 1905   42

4. From *Imperialism, the Highest Stage of Capitalism,*
    1916   44

5. From *The State and Revolution,* 1917   45

The Path to the Bolsheviks' Seizure of Power   **48**

6. From *The Tasks of the Proletariat in the Present
    Revolution (April Theses),* April 1917   49

7. From *Speech in Favor of the Resolution on the War,*
    April 27 (May 10), 1917   51

8. From *Resolution on the National Question,* May 1917   52

9. From *An Open Letter to the Delegates of the All-Russian
    Congress of Peasants' Deputies,* May 7 (29), 1917   53

10. From *The Political Situation,* July 10 (23), 1917   56

11. From *The Impending Catastrophe and How to Combat
     It,* September 10–14 (September 23–27), 1917   57

12. From *One of the Fundamental Questions of the
     Revolution,* September 27 (October 10), 1917   59

**2. The Monopolization of Power during the Civil
    War: 1917–1920**   **61**

Toward One-Party Power   **62**

13. From *To Workers, Soldiers, and Peasants!* October 25
     (November 7), 1917   62

14. From *Resolution of the Central Committee of the
     RSDLP(B) on the Opposition within the Central
     Committee,* November 2 (15), 1917   63

15. *Decree on the Arrest of the Leaders of the Civil War
     against the Revolution,* November 28 (December 11),
     1917   64

16. From *Draft Decree on the Dissolution of the
     Constituent Assembly,* January 6 (19), 1918   65

17. From *Speech to Propagandists on Their Way to the
     Provinces,* February 5, 1918   67

18. *Interview Granted to an* Izvestia *Correspondent in Connection with the Left Socialist-Revolutionary Revolt*, July 8, 1918   69

The Bolshevik Terror and the Stigmatization of Public Enemies   **71**

19. *Draft Resolution on Freedom of the Press*, November 4 (17), 1917   71

20. *Letter to G. I. Blagonravov and V. D. Bonch-Bruevich*, December 8 (21), 1917   73

21. *Telegram to V. L. Paniushkin*, June 15, 1918   74

22. *Letter to G. E. Zinoviev*, June 26, 1918   75

23. From *Report of the Council of People's Commissars on the Fifth All-Russian Congress of Soviets*, July 5, 1918   76

24. *Telegram to the Penza Gubernia Executive Committee of the Soviets*, August 19, 1918   77

25. From *Letter to Maxim Gorky*, September 15, 1919   78

Problems of War and World Revolution   **79**

26. *The Socialist Fatherland Is in Danger!* February 21, 1918   80

27. V. I. Lenin and others, From *Resolution on War and Peace*, March 8, 1918   82

28. From *Letter to the Workers and Peasants apropos of the Victory over Kolchak*, August 24, 1919   83

29. From *Letter to American Workers*, August 20, 1918   86

30. From *Speech at the Opening Session of the Congress*, March 2, 1919   88

31. From *"Left-Wing" Communism — an Infantile Disorder*, April–May 1920   89

32. From *Report on the International Situation and the Fundamental Tasks of the Communist International to the Second Congress of Comintern*, July 19, 1920   90

33. From *Political Report to the Ninth All-Russian Conference of the RCP(B)*, September 20, 1920   92

**War Communism and the Invention of a
Command Economy**   **94**

34. From *The Immediate Tasks of the Soviet Government*,
    March–April 1918 (published in *Pravda* on April 28,
    1918)   94

35. From *Organization of Food Detachments*, June 27,
    1918   97

36. From *Speech to the First All-Russian Congress of Land
    Departments, Poor Peasants' Committees, and
    Communes*, December 11, 1918   99

37. From *Political Report of the Central Committee to the
    Eighth All-Russian Conference of the RCP(B)*,
    December 2, 1919   101

**3. Threats to the Revolution: The Development
of the New Economic Policy**   **103**

**Disputes and Opposition in the Party,
1920–1921**   **104**

38. From *The Party Crisis*, January 21 (February 3),
    1921   104

39. *Summary of Lenin's Remarks at the Conference of the
    Delegates to the Tenth Congress of the RCP(B) —
    Supporters of the Platform of Ten*, March 13, 1921   106

40. From *Preliminary Draft Resolution of the Tenth
    Congress of the RCP on Party Unity*, March 1921   108

**Anti-Bolshevik Popular Uprisings and the Shift in
Policy**   **111**

41. From *Report on the Political Work of the Central
    Committee of the RCP(B) on Tenth Congress of the
    RCP(B)*, March 8, 1921   112

42. *Rough Draft of Theses Concerning the Peasants*,
    February 8, 1921   114

Lenin's Objective in the New Economic Policy   **115**

43. From *Report on the Substitution of a Tax in Kind for
    the Surplus Grain Appropriation System*, March 15,
    1921   115

44. *Draft Resolution on the Question of the New Economic
Policy for the Tenth Conference of the RCP(B)*, May 1921   119

45. V. I. Lenin and V. M. Molotov, *Telegram to All
Provincial and Regional Party Committees of the
RCP(B)*, July 30, 1921   123

46. From *The Political Report of the Central Committee of
the RCP(B) to the Eleventh Congress of the RCP(B)*,
March 27, 1922   125

Economic Policy under the NEP   **129**

47. From *Five Years of the Russian Revolution and the
Prospects of the World Revolution: Report to the Fourth
Congress of the Communist International*,
November 13, 1922   129

48. *Letter to Maxim Gorky*, December 6, 1921   134

The Institutionalization of a One-Party System   **135**

49. From *We Have Paid Too Much*, April 9, 1922   135

50. *Letter to I. V. Stalin*, July 17, 1922   139

Toward a Single Spiritual and Cultural System   **141**

51. *Letter to A. V. Lunacharsky,* May 6, 1921   142

52. *Letter to V. M. Molotov for the Politburo of the CC of
RCP(B)*, January 12, 1922   143

53. From *The Tasks of the Youth Leagues*, October 2, 1920   144

54. From *Letter to V. M. Molotov for the Members of the
CC of RCP(B)*, March 19, 1922   146

**4. The Sick Leader: De Facto Removal from
Power**   **150**

55. *Letter to Stalin for Politburo of RCP(B) CC*,
June 15, 1922   151

56. From *Letter to the Congress: Continuation of the
Notes*, December 24, 1922   152

57. *Letter to I. V. Stalin*, March 5, 1923   155

Lenin's Last Thoughts   **156**

58. From *On Co-operation*, January 4 and 6, 1923   157

59. From *The Question of Nationalities or
    "Autonomization,"* December 30, 1922   159

APPENDIXES

A Chronology of V. I. Lenin's Life (1870–1924)   162

Questions for Consideration   165

Selected Bibliography   166

Index   169

PART ONE

Introduction:
V. I. Lenin's Life
and Legacy

V. I. Lenin was born under a divine-right monarchy and died the leader of the world's first one-party state. He grew up in a rapidly expanding market economy and left behind an economic system in which the state was chief owner and employer. At the time of his death, Russia's recovery from World War I, the Russian Civil War, and the extreme economic policies Lenin initially instituted was incomplete. Yet power and authority had shifted decisively from wealthy elites to party officials in the new Soviet Republic. For some, Lenin's Russia embodied the promise of a new world that would be more just and prosperous than the liberal capitalist democracies were. For others, his rule signified a disastrous aberration in Russian and European history. However it is interpreted, Lenin's impact on the twentieth century is beyond dispute.

V. I. LENIN AND THE FOUNDING
OF THE SOVIET STATE

Lenin founded the Soviet state in October 1917 (November, new style)[1] and shaped its political processes. He was the first among the leading Bolsheviks to imagine its existence and the chief proponent of its creation. During five years of rule, he helped set its course and became its most vibrant and lasting human symbol. The system that he helped to construct later spread to Eastern and Central Europe, China, Indochina, North Korea, and Cuba. In addition, much of the developing world adopted forms of his one-party rule and state-managed economic life. In its heyday, the Soviet Union challenged America both militarily and technologically. After the collapse of the Soviet Union, communism still shapes the memory of more than half the world's population, many of whom still live in modified forms of Soviet-type political systems.

During his years in power, Lenin wielded near absolute influence over the Bolshevik inner circle. While Lenin lived, the Bolsheviks lauded him as a secular saint who set the country and the world on the path to socialism. After he died on January 21, 1924, his colleagues mummified him and exhibited his body under glass in a special mausoleum in Moscow, much to the horror of his wife and other members of his family. Afterward, his cult ran in the background of daily Soviet life, imposing meaning on the country's historical experience. Even the fall of Russian communism in 1991 failed to dislodge Lenin as a potent symbol of Russian pride.

Our objective in this book is to illuminate, on the basis of his own writings, Lenin's role as the initiator and architect of the Soviet system. These texts tell an important story. Lenin lived at a time when radio and film were in their infancy, and therefore the printed word had its maximum impact. Printed speeches, telegrams, letters, newspapers, and books were the primary means of communication. When Lenin wanted something done, he usually gave written instructions. Thus he left historians with a long paper trail that could be examined and used to explain how he gained and wielded the power to transform Russia and shape world history.

Soviet editions of Lenin's writings illustrate both his personal role in the development of Bolshevism and the country's sociopolitical evolution under his active leadership, which lasted until his first serious stroke in May of 1922. The editors of his *Collected Works*, including the final, fifth Soviet edition (*The Complete Collected Works*), selectively excluded more than 3,500 known documents and condensed and "corrected" included texts.[2] Selections of Lenin's writings, instructions, and orders published recently from hitherto secret archives provide an opportunity to amplify his official image and construct a more objective picture of the man and of the varied projects he sought to realize.

Lenin and his followers as a rule subordinated ideology to other concerns. In order to justify their abrupt abandonment of one course for another, they sometimes invoked Marx's dialectical notion that a clash of opposites yields a new synthesis. This does not mean that ideology meant nothing to Lenin, but only that his words cannot usually be understood apart from his actions. Therefore, we have chosen the following selections with Lenin's practical activity in mind. Readers of this book can consider whether Lenin discarded ideology when it suited him in the pursuit of power or merely showed the flexibility of a successful policymaker working within an ideological framework.

Lenin was something of a chameleon, and the documents offer a variegated picture of him as a theorist, a revolutionary, a state leader, and, finally, an invalid, shunted aside by his would-be successors. In some selections, he appears at his most persuasive, simplifying the tasks to be undertaken, justifying his actions with appeals to social justice, and promising to overcome all obstacles with a heady optimism. Such performances illuminate the influence he had over rank-and-file activists as well as over his colleagues, many of whom were powerful personalities and political figures with followings of their own. In other selections, Lenin speaks as a tough, authoritarian boss, forcing his will on his followers and dealing mercilessly with opponents and "class enemies." Exploring the text, readers can judge for themselves how ideological or personal Lenin's quest for power was, how popular or authoritarian his leadership was, how nationalistic or internationalist his ideology was, and how his vision of Russia's historical development unfolded.

THE RUSSIA OF LENIN'S YOUTH

Lenin grew up in a rebellious era. He was born Vladimir Ilich Ulyanov on April 10, 1870 (April 22, new style), in Simbirsk, a Volga port later renamed Ulyanovsk that became a site of pilgrimage for faithful communists after Lenin's death. Lenin was the third of six children (see Figure 1). His father was a school inspector, a post of considerable local prestige. Among educated professionals such as Lenin's father, the memory of Russia's humiliating defeat by Britain and France in the Crimean War (1853–1856) would have been painfully sharp. After the war, Tsar Alexander II (1818–1881), who reigned from 1855 to 1881, carried out the Great Reforms to address shortcomings revealed by the war. He abolished serfdom in 1861, freeing over twenty million peasants, who were near slaves, from the arbitrary personal, legal, and administrative power of their aristocratic, clerical, or royal owners. He created a judicial system with trial by jury and elective local and regional governmental institutions to provide schooling and other services. He instituted fiscal reform, a liberalization of censorship, and measures to improve and expand education at all levels and for all classes. The last of the Great Reforms, the Universal Military Service Statute of 1874, established a draft applicable to all males, although those with the least education served on active duty the longest (six years), while those with the most education served the least (six months).

The Great Reforms did not eliminate Russia's discriminatory ladder of hereditary class privilege: the social order of legal estates that set nobles, merchants, priests, and even lower-class city residents above peasants in law, education, and economic life. In an age of democratic reform, these inequalities lost whatever justification they had previously enjoyed. Nevertheless, they remained in place as a source of resentment for the vast majority of the population. In addition, the tsar retained his autocratic power as the source of national legislation and font of judicial authority, responsible only to God.

Despite considerable economic growth during the late nineteenth century, the Russian Empire lagged ever further behind Britain, France, and Germany. In 1870, the year of Lenin's birth, Russia's per capita gross domestic product ($1,023 per head in 1990 U.S. dollars) was 48 percent of Western Europe's; by 1900 it was only 39 percent ($1,218 per head); and in 1913 still no more than 40 percent ($1,488).[3] Russia also trailed Eastern Europe, though it outpaced Asia, much of Latin America, and Africa, where economic growth was stagnant. Furthermore, Russia's limited wealth was unevenly distributed geographically and in terms of nationality. The nation's borders extended to the Ottoman Empire (the future Turkey) and Afghanistan in the south; to China and the Pacific Ocean in the east; to the Arctic Ocean in the north; and to Germany, Austro-Hungary, and Romania in the west and southwest. European Russia, the region west of the Ural Mountains (including Poland and the Baltic nations) was generally more developed, while Central Asia and some other non-Russian regions remained almost untouched by economic development. Large parts of Russia, particularly European Russia, were becoming industrialized, so that by 1913 agriculture contributed just over half of the national income in the Empire.[4] In fact, the urban population of European Russia more than tripled between 1863 and 1913, and large cities grew at

Figure 1. *Lenin's Family Portrait, 1879*
Lenin is on the far right; Lenin's sister Maria, who took dictation for Lenin in
his last years, is seated on the knee of Lenin's mother, with Alexander, the
brother executed as a terrorist, standing in the back between his parents.
Prints and Photographs Division, Library of Congress, LC-USZ62-64899.

5

even greater rates. Moscow's population rose from 462,000 in 1863 to 1,762,000 in 1914, while St. Petersburg's population increased from 470,000 to 2,118,000 during the same period.[5] To radicals such as Lenin, the ostentatious displays of new bourgeois wealth in these great cities must have made the ordinary people's grinding poverty seem all the more unjust and irrational.

Meanwhile, the spread of education created a public likely to view the tsarist social order critically. The number of pupils in primary and secondary schools increased more than tenfold, from 955,000 in 1860 to 9,656,000 in 1914, and the number of students in higher educational institutions increased almost fifteenfold, from 8,500 in 1860 to 127,000 in 1913.[6] By 1914, more than 20 percent of those receiving a higher education were of peasant origins, up from a mere 3 percent in 1880.[7] Overall literacy remained generally low, but that too was changing. According to the 1897 census, 29 percent of men and 13 percent of women in the Empire were literate. This was roughly on a par with backward Spain in 1860 (30 percent male literacy and 20 percent female literacy).[8] Nevertheless, literacy among the young, particularly men, and among the urban population was rising rapidly. Literacy among army recruits rose from 19 percent in 1870 to 68 percent in 1913.[9] By 1910, more than three-quarters of the population of St. Petersburg, Russia's capital, was literate, as was more than two-thirds of Moscow's.[10] As a result, there was no shortage of volunteers to read simple political broadsides and newspapers aloud to others.

While historians still argue about whether prerevolutionary Russia would have failed economically if the Bolsheviks had not seized power, Russia faced grave political and economic challenges.[11] A portion of the educated elite opposed the autocracy even before the Great Reforms, and afterward their dissatisfaction that the liberated peasants were not given more land, outrage at widespread social injustice, and unfavorable comparisons with Western Europe fueled further dissent. In the 1870s, the autocracy's intellectual critics became known collectively as the intelligentsia, a word that entered the English language and came to refer to a coterie of highly educated, critically minded elites. In Lenin's youth, the intelligentsia was composed chiefly of two groups. One was the liberals, who dreamed of a Russian parliamentary democracy like that of England and worked for change in the new institutions of local government. The other was the populists, who sought an egalitarian society based on Russia's traditional peasant communes, the village councils of heads of households that periodically divided the farmland according to the number of working males in a household. The members of underground revolutionary organizations, the most radical among the populists, employed various means, including violence, to try to overthrow the autocracy or at least compel the tsar to carry out agrarian reform. In 1881, radical populists trying to force the government to accede to their demands assassinated Tsar Alexander II. In response, the tsar's son, Alexander III (1845–1894), who reigned from 1881 to 1894, rejected reform almost entirely. Some activists continued the struggle, including Lenin's older brother Alexander, who was hanged in 1887 for trying to assassinate the tsar.

The year his brother was arrested and executed, Lenin won a gold medal in his final exams at the gymnasium, an educational institution similar to the American high school, although pupils were younger when they entered. In August 1887, at the age of 17, Lenin began to study law at the University of Kazan, but was arrested for joining a radical group and expelled. Unable to continue his studies, he read his brother's books and studied Marxism, a revolutionary ideology and economic theory developed by German social theorists Karl Marx (1818–1883) and Friedrich Engels (1820–1895). At the time, Marxism was an ideology with adherents worldwide, including the members of the German Social Democratic Party (SPD), which in the 1890 national election received 1,472,000 votes. The SPD was reformist, not revolutionary, but its prestige was high after the party survived German Chancellor Otto von Bismarck's attempt to crush it in 1878. To the young Lenin and other Russian Marxists, European Marxism meant the SPD.

In 1891, Lenin was at last allowed to take the law examinations at St. Petersburg University. He passed and began work as an attorney in Samara, a scenic port town of Russians and Tatars on the Volga River. The beginning of Lenin's law career also marked the beginning of his revolutionary career.

LENIN AS REVOLUTIONARY

When Lenin took up politics, revolutionary activity was largely an avocation. He and others, however, gradually turned this avocation into a profession, a career open to talent. Active, ambitious young Russians chose revolutionary work over other occupations as a wager on the future. They sought power in part because, like Lenin, they felt they knew what to do with it. Early Russian Marxists imagined an industrial future for Russia led by the proletariat, or working class, and were encouraged by the signs of industrialization and urbanization that they saw around them. Populism and Marxism, despite their inherent utopianism, were virtual opposites. Populists valued morally committed individuals as agents of change. Populists preferred social reform to political reform. Marxists claimed a science of historical development with social classes rather than individuals as actors in the movement for political reform. Notably, Marxists disavowed terrorism. Most, including Lenin, stressed the need for state power. Populists wished to spare Russia the ills of capitalist industrialization. Although opposed to capitalism itself, Marxists welcomed capitalist industrialization as the fourth of Marx's five socioeconomic stages of development (primitive, slave-holding, feudal, capitalist, and communist) and thus a necessary step in the development of a communist society. Lenin and his fellow Marxists believed a proletarian revolution would usher in the final phase of human development, a classless communist society.

Eventually, Lenin diverged from Marx and Engels with respect to the stages of history. Marx and Engels argued that every society had to go through a feudal and then a bourgeois (capitalist) stage to reach proletarian rule: Lenin wanted Russia to advance more rapidly. Although the proletariat constituted only a tiny minority of the population, Lenin hoped to use the state to realize the promise of proletarian revolution. At first, Lenin expected backward Russia to be rescued by revolutions in more advanced countries (Documents 29–32). When these revolutions did not materialize, he was eager to create a socialist society in Russia alone (Document 34). He assumed the proletarian revolution would replace inequity and suffering with plentitude and social justice. Lenin presumably sought power for these ends, but he also seems to have sought power as an end in itself.

How did this provincial upstart gain sway over Russian Marxism? He did so gradually, but with a single-minded determination to advance his cause. Lenin began organizing workers in the early 1890s, while writing antipopulist pamphlets and working with Marxist organizations. He was arrested in December 1895 and exiled to the Krasnoiarsk region, in western Siberia. Nadezhda Konstantinovna Krupskaia (1869–1939), a comrade in local Marxist organizing in St. Petersburg, gained permission from the government to join Lenin as his fiancée. They soon married as required under the agreement that permitted her to join a political exile. Krupskaia supported Lenin as a skilled and loyal helpmate throughout his life (Figure 2).

Figure 2. *Lenin and Krupskaia in the Garden at Gorki (undated, probably 1922)*
This private country estate, which was named Gorki in the nineteenth century long before the writer Maxim Gorky adopted his pseudonym, was nationalized in 1918 and turned into a museum ("Lenin's Gorki") in 1938.
Prints and Photographs Division, Library of Congress, LC-USZ62-73312.

While in Siberia, Lenin finished his first book, a semi-academic study, *The Development of Capitalism in Russia*. Published under the pseudonym "Ilin," the book was a success, earning Lenin a reputation as an economist. His thesis that capitalism was transforming rural Russia by dividing the peasants into rich and poor seemed indisputable to many young people since change was evident everywhere. The more energetic and successful peasants were adopting new implements and tools, such as iron plows and harrows, and improving their houses with brick stoves and tin roofs.[12] They even donned machine-made clothing. The populists bewailed the corruption of rural life, but Marxists applauded this confirmation of Marx's schema in which the rise of capitalism foreshadowed the future proletarian revolution.

Lenin served out his exile, and in 1901, he and Krupskaia joined other Marxists abroad. In the same year, Vladimir changed his surname from Ulyanov to Lenin, after the Lena goldfields, once famous for their labor strife, and the Lena River, which flows thousands of miles from its source near Lake Baikal in Siberia to the Laptev Sea in the Arctic Ocean. While abroad, he helped found the Marxist newspaper *Iskra* (*The Spark*) and published his seminal pamphlet *What Is to Be Done?* (1902, see Document 2).

Lenin saw *Iskra* as a platform from which to organize a group that shared his ideas: He articulated those ideas in *What Is to Be Done?* In roughly a hundred pages, he envisaged an elite conspiratorial party of professional revolutionaries leading the masses to socialism. He expressed his faith that a few "wise men" could lead the proletariat in the coming revolution. Within months, Lenin led his own faction to victory at the Second Congress of the fledgling Russian Social-Democratic Workers' Party. At the Second Congress, which took place in Brussels and London during the summer of 1903, Lenin's faction, which favored an underground elitist party over a mass party outvoted their opponents, who were dubbed Mensheviks (the minority), and took the name of Bolsheviks (the majority). The tags stuck, although the Bolsheviks soon lost the majority in the party.

Russian Marxists had every reason to expect a bourgeois revolution in Russia, but the Revolution of 1905, which was provoked in part by an unsuccessful war with Japan (February 1904–August 1905), was something of a surprise with its peasant uprisings, labor strife, and radical character. The Revolution of 1905 developed in two phases. First, a diverse group opposing the tsar and encompassing much of the political spectrum took form. This group included moderate liberals, the Socialist-Revolutionary Party (SR), heirs to revolutionary populism, and the Russian Social-Democratic Workers' Party (SD) on the left, as well as the non-Russian nationalities, particularly Ukrainians, Poles, Georgians, the Baltic peoples, and Finns. Pressure on the autocracy from this coalition grew when tsarist troops fired on workers peacefully demonstrating near the Winter Palace on "Bloody Sunday," January 9, 1905 (January 22, new style), and Russia lost the war with Japan. A general strike followed in October, and a Soviet of Workers' Deputies formed to manage affairs in St. Petersburg and elsewhere. The soviets, a remarkable innovation of revolutionary politics, appeared in various cities and were informal assemblies of workers and representatives from trade unions with a sprinkling of radical political activists. The delegates were chiefly men, although a few women did participate.

In the second phase of the Revolution of 1905, the opposition coalition fractured in response to concessions from Tsar Nicholas II (1868–1918, reigned 1894–1917), the moderates' fear of social unrest, and the divergence of radical and liberal demands. In the October Manifesto, the document detailing his concessions to the opposition, the tsar promised basic civil freedoms as well as a representative assembly—the State Duma—to approve all laws. These promises satisfied enough moderates to weaken the opposition. As the revolutionary coalition fragmented, counterrevolutionary forces rallied. The SR and the SD still pressed for political and social change, but the liberal Constitutional Democratic Party (KD, or the Cadet Party) feared violence and sought moderate reform. Soon afterward, the more conservative Octobrist Party formed and promised to cooperate with the government. The far right also mobilized with the support of the autocracy and some members of the Russian Orthodox clergy. The trade union movement, which was still largely independent of any political grouping, became isolated, and its pleas for an eight-hour workday were ignored.

Lenin and Krupskaia returned to Russia in November 1905 to take advantage of the liberties enacted by the October Manifesto. Lenin now headed his own group of radical organizers and intellectuals, and he began writing for the Bolshevik newspaper *Novaia zhizn'* (New Life), which appeared legally under the relaxed censorship following the revolution. Yet the gains of 1905 proved illusory. Tsar Nicholas II decided not to honor the October Manifesto, and in early 1906 he announced a more limited electoral system than that document promised. Although two State Dumas were democratically elected, one in 1906 and another a year later, the tsar dissolved both for being too radical. After the dissolution of the Second Duma in June 1907, he limited the franchise and the representation of the nationalities; the prospects for revolution dimmed. The lesson that Lenin drew from the failure of the Revolution of 1905 was that Marxists should lead workers and peasants to "a real and decisive victory," since the bourgeois liberals had failed to do so.

In the aftermath of 1905, Lenin impatiently sought to consolidate his Bolshevik faction of the Russian Social-Democratic Workers' Party and set its separate course. In the fall of 1907, after the party's Fifth Congress, he contemplated a split with rival Marxists. He had attended

several congresses at which he was outvoted and Mensheviks criticized his idea of a worker-peasant alliance, his conspiratorial politics,
and his financing of Bolshevik operations by bank robberies and other
unscrupulous methods.[13] Lenin and Krupskaia left Russia for Helsinki
in November 1907 and would not return for nearly a decade, after
Europe had been engulfed in World War I and the tsar overthrown.

While abroad, Lenin again used his time well, gaining repute
among a small but influential circle of activists through his writing and
his furious advocacy of his views in émigré circles. In January 1912,
he organized the Sixth Party Conference in Prague, in which only
Bolsheviks took part. After that his group emerged as a separate
party that five years later took the official name of the Russian Social-
Democratic Workers' Party (Bolshevik). In 1912, Lenin also oversaw
the founding of *Pravda* (The Truth), the legally published Russian
daily that would become his voice. Lenin's control over the Bolsheviks
was still shaky on occasion, but his stature continued to grow, in part
because of his writing. In 1916, he wrote *Imperialism, the Highest
Stage of Capitalism* (Document 4) and in July 1917, *The State and Revolution* (Document 5). In the first, he argued that imperialist wars
would bring down European capitalism. In the second, written in Russian Finland, he described a great social and economic revolution carried out by the state, a state that he imagined as much more
democratic than the one that he would actually help to create.

WORLD WAR I AND THE RUSSIAN REVOLUTION

World War I was a tragic struggle in which Russia joined with Britain,
France, and other nations against Germany, Austro-Hungary, Turkey,
and Bulgaria. Each side had its reasons for fighting, but the longer the
war continued, the less compelling these reasons seemed to many
Russians. The Russian Army suffered serious defeats at the outset,
stabilized the front in late 1915 and early 1916, and then embarked on
an unsuccessful offensive that produced massive casualties and widespread discontent in the remainder of 1916 and early 1917.

After the outbreak of the war, Lenin and Krupskaia moved to neu-
tral Switzerland, a center of antiwar activity. Before World War I, most
European socialists and their Social Democratic parties expected to
oppose any European war, but when the war actually began, they supported their governments. Lenin was among the minority who opposed the war as a slaughter from which the workers had nothing to

gain. In Switzerland, he fumed against the treachery of European Social Democrats who had supported their governments despite their earlier vows to prevent a war by urging all workers to go on strike. Russian socialists split on the issue of supporting the war effort but not on party lines. Most Socialist Revolutionaries and Mensheviks supported a defensive war effort and sought a negotiated settlement. Some in each party, however, argued that the war could only be ended by revolutions in the warring states. Even many Bolsheviks argued for Russia's defense against imperialist Germany. Lenin, however, did not waver in his demand that socialists undermine the military efforts of their own countries. He believed European workers would eventually rise against their governments, turning the world war into a civil war.

The February Revolution of 1917 (which actually took place in March according to our calendar), in which the tsarist government was overthrown by a spontaneous uprising that began with food riots, confirmed Lenin's prognosis in *Imperialism* (Document 4) that the world war weakened capitalism. Not only did the Russian autocracy find few defenders in view of the unpopular war, but the foreign governments that Lenin believed might have propped up the old regime were unable to do so. When protests spread, the Russian police lacked the force to reestablish order, and the army and the Cossacks, special army units of hereditary frontier soldiers who traditionally suppressed disorder, lacked the will. The autocracy bungled the crisis, and power passed to a Provisional Government composed of the Duma and a revived Soviet, now including representatives of army units as well as workers, trade unionists, and leaders from socialist parties. The tsar abdicated, and Russia became a republic. The Provisional Government was centrist, except for A. F. Kerensky, a socialist on the Petrograd Soviet's Executive Committee, who broke ranks to become minister of justice. Conceived in a liberal and democratic spirit, the Provisional Government instituted considerable reform with respect to individual rights and the rights of women. Nevertheless, it squandered its authority by continuing the war, mismanaging the economy, delaying land reform, alienating restive nationalities, and postponing elections for a constituent assembly or constitutional convention. In the Provisional Government, power drifted to Kerensky, who became the minister-president and ruled as a virtual dictator during the summer and fall of 1917.

The February Revolution raised expectations that went unsatisfied. After an ill-conceived military offensive in July 1917, the Russian Army began to disintegrate. Living conditions in Russian cities deteriorated.

Workers' demands for control over their workplaces went unmet. In the countryside, peasants began to seize land from private estates, the Orthodox Church, and the tsar's family. Soldiers, exposed to antiwar propaganda from Bolsheviks and others, deserted, hoping for a share of whatever land was being seized.

While the Provisional Government floundered, Lenin and his Bolsheviks became the most visible organized alternative to the status quo, winning new influence in city government, trade unions, and, most importantly, the soviets that were created in all cities, in many counties, and in the army. Lenin had long sought a centralized, secretive political party. Still living in Switzerland, he hoped to use that party to take power in a socialist revolution with both workers' and peasants' support. He must have been delighted when the German government agreed to send him home by train with other antiwar émigrés in the hope that they would undermine the Russian war effort (see Figure 3). Lenin reached Petrograd (until 1914, known as St. Petersburg) on April 3 (16). There he shocked Bolsheviks and others by denouncing the war and the Provisional Government. The next day he presented his famous "April Theses" (Document 6) to two party meetings. In this document, he urged the transfer of all power to the soviets. Initially, Lenin's Bolsheviks were a minority in the soviets, but by September 1917, they controlled the soviets in Petrograd, Russia's capital, and in its second largest city, Moscow.

The Bolsheviks seized power in the October Revolution on October 25–26 (November 7–8), 1917, in Petrograd in what amounted to a coup d'état. On October 7 (October 20) Lenin had returned from Finland, where he had been hiding since July, and convinced the Bolshevik Central Committee of the need to act quickly. The Bolsheviks had gained a majority in the soviet in Petrograd, but a Congress of Soviets was scheduled to meet in late October and Lenin wanted to present it with a fait accompli. On the night of October 24, the Military Revolutionary Committee of the Petrograd Soviet sent the army units and workers' militias loyal to it into action. Opposition was feeble or nonexistent. Kerensky fled the capital, and efforts to organize resistance to the Bolshevik seizure of power failed. Resistance in Moscow was greater, but that, too, was quickly suppressed. Why, among the handful of established parties, did Lenin's party succeed while others failed? Historians' explanations range from those that emphasize Lenin's and the Bolsheviks' skill and the comparative ineptness of their rivals and the Provisional Government to those that seek answers beyond the actions of individual historical actors and see an explanation in the extent of Russia's problems, its lack of democratic

Figure 3. *Lenin's Passport Photo, 1917*
The passport photo Lenin used to travel from Switzerland after the February
Revolution to Petrograd (St. Petersburg) in April 1917.
Yanker poster collection, Prints and Photographs Division, Library of Congress, LC-
USZC4-8334.

traditions, its weak civil society, and its long authoritarian rule. Re-
gardless of the explanation that appears most satisfying, neither leadership nor tradition can be comfortably ignored. When the Russian
Revolution began, the Bolsheviks were weak. Other groups initially

enjoyed the support of various social strata, but they did not articulate specific programs to address demands for bread, land, peace, and the rights of nationalities within the empire. Only the Bolsheviks, under Lenin's direction, did so, however demagogically. At the expense of their rivals, they won support from the ordinary people, for whom these problems were the chief concern, particularly people in the cities and in the trade unions.[14] By the autumn of 1917, in fact, the Bolshevik Party seemed to be the only alternative to the Provisional Government, in part because all the other major parties had participated in the government at one point or another. The SRs and Mensheviks in the Petrograd Soviet, who refused to advocate "soviet power," saw their influence wane, while the Bolsheviks invoked the insults of class, poverty, and social rank so endemic in imperial Russia to gain support. Moreover, the most influential party, the SR, split into two factions. One faction, the Left SRs, chose to back the Bolsheviks, while the remaining SRs and the other parties opposed them. In addition, the Bolsheviks co-opted key SR slogans, notably one about transferring land from wealthy landowners and the church to peasants as private property. Promising soldiers, peasants, and workers "land, bread, and peace," Lenin and his followers outflanked their rivals.

Lenin had another advantage. He conceived of his party chiefly as a quasimilitary force for the forcible seizure of power and for the application of that power to transform society. His party was chiefly neither a forum for different views nor the voice of a particular constituency. It was a means to hasten history and to establish socialism in Russia by violent means. Lenin had imagined various scenarios in which this might happen in his most famous semi-theoretical writings, such as *What Is to Be Done?* (Document 2) and *The State and Revolution* (Document 5). In October 1917, he acted upon them.

Was Lenin seeking personal power or the power to transform Russia and the world? For him the two were probably inseparable. He believed he knew best how to win state power and how to use it. History confirms Lenin's judgment on the first count, if not on the second. His apparent success in each, however, won the loyalty of able associates from Leon Trotsky to Josef Stalin, who would help Lenin secure Bolshevik rule despite their own personal animosities and disagreements.

Once in power, the Bolsheviks established a government responsible to the party, not to the soviets. Lenin headed the Council of People's Commissars, and Trotsky headed the People's Commissariat of Foreign Affairs. Lenin announced decrees on peace (peace without annexations or indemnities), land (nationalization of all landed estates, with their moveable property to be given to the peasants to use, but not to own), and the formation of a new Central Executive Committee of the Soviets (with participation by the Left SRs). Jointly, this committee and the periodic congresses of soviets would officially play the role of a legislature. Power quickly shifted to soviets in the rest of the country and to Bolsheviks where they had majorities. The Bolsheviks called an election for the Constituent Assembly as they had promised, but when the Assembly convened on January 5(18), 1918, the Socialist-Revolutionary Party (SRs) had a clear majority. Although the Left SRs supported the Bolsheviks, the delegates were chiefly from the more moderate SR faction that did not. In order to maintain and solidify their power, the Bolsheviks abolished the Constituent Assembly (Document 16) and began to rule by themselves, first through the soviets with the support of the Left SRs, and then entirely on their own.

BOLSHEVIK RULE AND THE NEW SOVIET STATE

Lenin's impact on Russian and world history depends chiefly on the unique party state that he created. Bolshevik rule did not initially preclude the existence of other political parties, but Lenin never gave opponents free reign. From November 1917 to March 1918, some Left Socialist-Revolutionaries occupied secondary positions in Lenin's government. Recognition of "soviet power"—the power of the elected soviets, particularly in Petrograd and Moscow—was a condition of a political party's legality from the outset. This precluded multiparty politics from the beginning because the bourgeois parties were never part of the soviets and the socialist parties, except for the Left Socialist-Revolutionaries, walked out of the Second All-Russian Congress of Soviets in protest when the Bolsheviks took power. The Bolsheviks soon banned all rival parties in any case. On November 28, 1917, Lenin signed a decree of the Council of People's Commissars outlawing the Constitutional Democratic Party as a party of "enemies of people" (Document 15). In 1918–1920, the suppression of other political parties followed, and in 1921, all parties except the Bolshevik Party were outlawed.

After seizing power, Lenin and his followers transformed the Bolshevik Party first into a guiding force inside the institutions of the new state, then into the government itself, and finally into an authoritarian institution encompassing the entire society. The ultimate power in the party resided in the periodic party congresses. In between party congresses the Central Committee* was the ruling authority. Under Lenin's direct leadership and by the decision of the Eighth Party Congress in March 1919, the highest power in the country was lodged in three small standing committees under the Central Committee. These were the Political Bureau (Politburo), on which the very top leaders sat; the Organizational Bureau (Orgburo), which was responsible for party organizing and appointments down to even the provincial level; and the Secretariat, which was responsible for carrying out the instructions of the Orgburo. It was important, however, for Lenin and his colleagues to take the next step to ensure the effective control of the whole society by the top party hierarchy. This consisted of the complete subordination of all party members, including those in very responsible positions, to the top leadership in the Politburo and to the sole leader, Lenin himself.

Under Lenin, every effort was made to mask the party's hegemony over the state. Lenin and the party continued to maintain strict secrecy about most important party decisions and about government decisions that originated in the party elite and not in appropriate government agencies. At the same time, however, Lenin and his supporters extolled the Communist Party's leading role in the state as the "greatest accomplishment" of the "proletarian dictatorship." The Bolsheviks officially changed their party's name to the All-Russian Communist Party (Bolsheviks) at the Seventh Party Congress in March 1918. The elite party was the core of the new centralized system of political power constructed under Lenin's leadership. Party leaders filled key roles in the government, which had a subordinate role to the party. Lenin saw this arrangement as an important condition for a centralized administration crowned by his own person. In his time, the party leadership ruled the chief governmental institutions from within. Subordinate agencies in the provinces operated similarly. "We are the state," Lenin informed delegates to the Eleventh Party Congress in early 1922.[15]

Such a system of partly covert power excluded formal checks and balances, precluded legislative restrictions on party actions, and ignored the would-be rights of citizens. Politics for Lenin was always

---

*The Bolsheviks probably took the term *central committee* from the Central Committee of the National Guard of the Paris Commune of 1870. The first central committee was elected at the first congress of the Russian Social-Democratic Workers' Party in 1898.

infused with class, and he was pitiless toward the "class enemy," a term he applied to most of those who tried to thwart him. Yet Lenin and the Bolsheviks did not invent class hatred, which had long been part of the underground culture of Russian revolutionaries and was expressed by ordinary people in both the February and October revolutions.[16] Lenin and the Bolsheviks mobilized this anger and used it, but they did not create it, even though their successful seizure of power may well have depended on it. Among the Bolsheviks, Lenin took the lead in ordering the arrest and execution of political opponents and those who rebelled against him personally (Documents 21 and 22).

Lenin did not jettison the protocols and morality of European society in a vacuum. Many millions had died in a vicious struggle for world power among the great capitalist nations in World War I and in smaller wars such as the Russo-Japanese War (1904–1905) and the South African, or Boer, War (1899–1902). When violating norms of European behavior, whether by taking hostages or shooting priests, Lenin would cite World War I and the hypocrisy of bourgeois Europe as justification for his actions. The logic that led him and the Bolsheviks to see politics as class war also led them to anticipate, and even to desire, civil war. When they embarked on their revolutionary adventure, they expected to ignite a worldwide struggle that would bring the advanced proletariats of Western Europe and America to their side. They were also prepared to challenge world capitalism and the Russian bourgeoisie. Lenin attributed the Bolsheviks' revolutionary victory to World War I in a speech given at the Seventh Party Congress in March 1918. "Individual imperialists," he wrote, "had no time to bother with us, solely because the whole of the great social, political, and military might of modern world imperialism was split by internecine war into two groups."[17]

Yet opposition to Bolshevik rule arose in many areas soon after the October Revolution, and the great capitalist nations were quick to support this opposition, even before the end of World War I. This opposition soon gave way to civil war. A revolt of the Don Cossacks in December 1917 led to the formation of a volunteer army that drove the Bolsheviks from the Don region and the Northern Caucasus in the first half of 1918. This army would be only one of several "White" armies that would encircle the Bolshevik Republic. The terms *white* and *red* were borrowed from the French Revolution, during which white was the color of the French monarchy and red was the color of supporters of the revolution in its radical phase. In Russia, these terms appeared in 1917 and were used often after the Bolsheviks' seizure of power to describe the Bolsheviks and their opponents. As the Civil War raged, the Germans sought to control Ukraine and the Baltic region, while the British, French, Americans, and Japanese landed small numbers of troops in the Soviet Far East. The British and French also sent troops to the north. The Allies acted, at least officially, to protect Allied stores, but the Japanese were clearly interested in annexing large portions of Siberia and augmented their troops in the Soviet Far East. In addition, the British and French aided White forces in Ukraine and the Caucasus. Yet in this struggle, as in the initial struggle for power, the Bolsheviks proved better organized than their divided opponents and had the advantage of holding the center of the country.[18]

During the Civil War, Poland, Finland, Lithuania, Latvia, and Estonia gained independence, but other nationalities that sought to escape Soviet rule did not fare so well. Non-Bolshevik governments appeared briefly in the Crimea, on the Don River, and in Central Asia, but these soon succumbed to Soviet might, as did the more durable independent states in Azerbaijan, Armenia, and Georgia.

The brutality of the civil war that Lenin and his colleagues predicted and partly provoked was used to justify their militarization of social and economic life. Replying to charges that the Bolsheviks had "renounced democracy" and that the Politburo was too secretive, Lenin told the Eighth Party Congress in March 1919, "We, as the militant organ of a militant party, in time of civil war, cannot work in any other way."[19] The Civil War raged for almost three years, during which the Bolsheviks' fortunes rose and fell. Even with victory finally in hand, Lenin felt that Soviet Russia was surrounded and infiltrated by enemies. "The enemy is lurking in wait for the Soviet Republic at every step," he told the Ninth Party Congress in early April 1920.[20]

WAR COMMUNISM: IDEOLOGY OR PRAGMATISM?

The Bolsheviks' economic policies reflected notions of class war and the assumption that all but workers and perhaps the least prosperous peasants would oppose them. The policies that came to be known as War Communism arose in the fall of 1918 as the Bolsheviks sought to both provide for the new Red Army and destroy the capitalist system and its supporters among the well-to-do peasants, the so-called kulaks, whom they believed to be a bulwark of the old order. War Communism began formally with the decree of the Council of People's Commissars on January 11, 1919, forbidding the private sale of grain. The government prohibited all private transactions and requisitioned grain and fodder, often taking the peasants' seed and supplies needed for livestock and spring planting, as well as the food they needed for their own sustenance. A black market soon developed, and the government tried to suppress it, thereby destroying the monetary link between country and city. A new phase of war communism commenced in the spring of 1920 after the defeat of three White generals ended widespread organized opposition to Bolshevik authority.

With victory in sight, the Bolsheviks faced the problem of whether to extend War Communism or rely on other mechanisms besides the state to structure economic and social life.[21] The Bolsheviks chose the more ideologically consistent option. The Ninth Party Congress (March–April 1920) adopted the plan of having the military run industry and transportation. A wave of decrees followed, substituting military discipline and orders from above for the already weakened monetary system as the chief motor of economic activity.

The verdict on the militarization of life in the new republic was not long in coming. Within a year, Lenin was forced to compromise in the face of a terrible famine as well as strikes and anti-Bolshevik agitation among workers, the intelligentsia, and white-collar employees. Peasants responded to government seizures of their crops by reducing the size of their plantings. Workers went on strike, and acts of disobedience were widespread in the winter of 1920–1921 and spring of 1921. Opposition culminated in the anti-Bolshevik uprising in March 1921 at the Petrograd naval base of Kronstadt, once a center of pro-Bolshevik fervor. The mutinous sailors demanded new elections to the soviets, various democratic freedoms for workers' and left-wing political parties, and an end to the limits on small-scale economic activity, including the sale of grain and handicrafts.

Lenin was already considering replacing forced requisition with a fixed tax on agricultural production, and the rebellion convinced him to act. At the Tenth Party Congress (March 1921), he proposed to substitute a fixed tax in kind for forced requisitioning, something Trotsky had suggested a year earlier and which party members now understood as a limited effort to placate peasants. The need to renew the economic nexus between city and countryside was also widely recognized. Party leaders understood that the peasants would not produce sufficient food for the cities or the army unless they could sell or trade their products and purchase something of value with the proceeds. Lenin therefore tried to reestablish a measure of commodity exchange, and accepted for the moment private property in handicraft production, light and midsized industry, and trade. This pragmatic reversal of policy was a success. Markets revived, money regained some value, peasants began to produce a surplus to sell in order to buy manufactured goods, and a strata of small entrepreneurs arose to effect such exchanges. The economy recovered, and the diverse policies that sparked this revival were called the New Economic Policy (NEP). The middlemen who helped to make the system work were scorned by the Bolsheviks as bourgeois profiteers and were contemptuously called Nepmen.

LENIN'S LAST ACTIVE YEARS: THE NEW ECONOMIC POLICY AND OTHER INNOVATIONS

Lenin was apprehensive lest the NEP become permanent and reduce his and the party's power, and he suppressed all opposition that might gain support from a more diverse economic life. He made two key decisions at the Tenth Party Congress in 1921. One involved crushing the Workers' Opposition, a group in the Bolshevik Party that promoted independent trade unions. The other decision, the banning of all party "factions," made it virtually impossible for those who opposed his leadership to organize in preparation for party congresses. The next year saw the exile of many noncommunist intellectuals and the trial of the leaders of the Socialist-Revolutionary Party. In the case of the Socialist-Revolutionaries, Lenin was forced to forgo applying the death penalty due to opposition from the international socialist movement, but he bitterly regretted the cost of this decision. "We have paid too much," he wrote in *Pravda*, the party newspaper, on April 11, 1922[22] (see Document 49). A month earlier, Lenin had expressed his impatience with the entire New Economic Policy at the Eleventh Party Congress in March 1922: "For a year we have been retreating. On behalf of the Party we must now call a halt. The purpose pursued by the retreat has been achieved."[23] Perhaps, as he felt his health failing, he wished to force a more rapid pace of change. In any case, he had long expected the state, not the market, to shape Russian economic life.

Lenin intended to use the state for social engineering, and he was not about to forgo culture as a means for social change. By 1917, he had rejected Marx's view that a socialist revolution was possible only after the proletariat had become the majority in the nation and had

Figure 4. *Lenin Holding a Copy of* Pravda *in His Study, October 1918*
Lenin in his study holding the chief party newspaper, *Pravda*. Lenin used
Pravda, the official organ of the Central Committee of the Bolshevik Party, to
impart his views and shape policy.
Prints and Photographs Division, Library of Congress, LC-USZ62-64916.

mastered the treasures of civilization. Instead, he adopted the strategy of some militant Russian revolutionaries of the 1870s and 1880s, who had hoped to seize power first and then win over the common people.[24] With this approach in mind, Lenin asked, "Why could not we first create such prerequisites of civilization in our country as the expulsion of the landowners and the Russian capitalists, and then start moving toward socialism?" Indeed, he continued, "Why cannot we begin by first achieving the prerequisites for that definite level of culture in a revolutionary way, and then, with the aid of the workers' and peasants' government and the Soviet System, proceed to overtake the other nations?"[25] This appeal echoed the thoughts of some Russian mystical thinkers such as Dostoevsky, who also expected Russia to demonstrate its superiority over other nations. Although Lenin handled issues involving literature and the arts more gingerly than he handled the economy, his inclination was to control everything.

Lenin approached foreign policy similarly, although in this case he seemed to juggle two incompatible ideas. One involved promotion of an international, or at least European, socialist revolution that would include anti-imperialist liberation movements in the colonial world. The other was to establish normal diplomatic and economic relations with capitalist nations even if the precondition for such relations was peaceful coexistence. Each idea was embodied in a different government institution. The Communist International, or Comintern, was created in 1919 to promote world revolution. The People's Commissariat of Foreign Affairs, which succeeded the Ministry of Foreign Affairs of the Provisional Government, sought normal diplomatic relations with capitalist countries. Lenin moved easily back and forth between the two institutions. Perhaps for him there was no discrepancy between their contrasting objectives since their duality represented a dialectic in which support for normal relations did not conflict with the advancement of world revolution, but complemented it. Lenin and his closest fellows, however, gave priority to the Comintern. *Pravda* published a cartoon soon after Lenin's death that illuminated the rivalry between the chairman of the Executive Committee of the Comintern, G. E. Zinoviev, and the People's Commissar for Foreign Affairs, G. V. Chicherin: While Zinoviev fulminated against the imperialists, Chicherin looked on horrified.[26]

With no successful revolutions being waged in the West, Lenin sought to gain security through diplomacy. His first important diplomatic success was the 1921 trade agreement with Great Britain that conferred de facto recognition of the Soviet Union and ended the country's isolation. His second success occurred at the conference on the reconstruction of postwar Europe held in Genoa, Italy, in April 1922. Lenin's ambiguous policy of participating in a meeting of capitalist states he sought to undermine succeeded. The Soviet Union avoided repayment of loans from the tsarist and provisional governments and signed the Treaty of Rapallo (a suburb of Genoa) with Germany. The two outcast nations established normal diplomatic relations, repudiated mutual debts and claims for reparations, and promised economic cooperation. A secret provision established military cooperation, which continued for a time even after Hitler took power. Though Genoa was a failure for the Allies, Russia divided the capitalist world and gained a surreptitious ally.

Soviet policy toward the nations and peoples of the former empire resembled Soviet foreign policy. The revolutionaries promised the nationalities of the former Russian empire self-determination, but the Soviet government under Lenin's authority used every means to keep the empire together under Russian control. Lenin and the Bolsheviks were willing to consider various forms of self-determination, but only within a unitary state.[27] In this respect, all the arguments and discussions of nationality policy under Lenin were secondary to the main issue of whether to reconstitute the empire, a question that Lenin and the other Bolshevik leaders had already resolved in the affirmative.

LENIN'S DECLINE

By 1922, after four years in power and many more of revolutionary struggle, Lenin had gathered around himself a group of able administrators and powerful personalities. Five stood out as possible successors. L. D. Trotsky (1879–1940), a key figure in 1905 and 1917, the architect of the victory in the Civil War and creator of the Red Army, was reckoned by many as second only to Lenin. He was a brilliant intellectual, and a gifted writer and speaker, whose brashness earned him many enemies—I. V. Stalin (1878–1953) among them. Stalin was not a leading figure in 1917, but his energy, administrative talent, cunning, and skill in bureaucratic infighting soon brought him to the top of the Bolshevik hierarchy. After the October Revolution, he became people's commissar for nationalities (1917–1922) and commissar for state control (1919–1923). In April 1922, he became the party's general secretary, with the power to assign party officials to different posts and hence to build a personal following. He alone among the Bolshevik leadership was a member both of the Politburo, the small standing committee with less than ten members that partly supplanted the Central Committee, and the Orgburo, the bureau of the Central Committee that directed organizational work.

More publicly visible than Stalin were two leaders who had questioned Lenin's decision to seize power in 1917, G. E. Zinoviev (1883–1936) and L. B. Kamenev (1883–1936). Lenin forgave them for this, but in the struggle for power after Lenin's death, Trotsky derided them in his essay "Lessons of October" (November 1924). Zinoviev, a fiery orator, was head of the Petrograd Soviet in December 1917, the first chairman of the Executive Committee of the Communist International from 1919, and a full member of the Politburo from 1921. Kamenev was chairman of the Moscow Soviet from 1918 and deputy chairman, or vice premier, of the Bolshevik government (officially named the Council of People's Commissars). The youngest of this group of the most promising leaders was N. I. Bukharin (1888–1938), an economist and gifted ideologue. In December 1917, Bukharin became editor of *Pravda*, the official party newspaper. He also became a leader of the Communist International in the late 1920s. Of the five, Stalin would prove the cleverest, and once in power, he would murder his rivals. The other major player in the drama of Lenin's decline was Lenin's wife, Krupskaia, who was active in education and in women's affairs, but held no important government posts. She became both nurse and secretary to the ailing leader.

In May 1922, Lenin suffered his first major stroke. Two additional stokes in December were followed by a general physical decline. With his strength failing, from December 25, 1922, to January 4, 1923, he dictated his so-called political testament (Document 57). In this testament, Lenin criticized Stalin's rudeness, intolerance, and arbitrariness, and suggested shifting him to a position less important than general secretary. He had recently opposed Stalin's efforts to reduce the autonomy of the nationalities. More important was Lenin's clash with Stalin over the limits placed on Lenin's activity. Stalin had placed Lenin under virtual house arrest on the pretext of protecting Lenin's health (see Figure 5). Given this background, Lenin's comments about Stalin may reflect irritability and anger more than a sudden desire to warn the party of impending danger. Lenin found fault with all of his colleagues and did not certify any as a suitable replacement during his protracted illness. The fact that he criticized his entire circle suggests that perhaps he was less interested in saving the party from Stalin, which he might have done by speaking more directly, than in expressing his general distress.

Some scholars have argued that, in his last few months, Lenin began reevaluating his entire program and even formulated a plan to redirect Soviet society on a less authoritarian course.[28] But a study of the texts produced during his decline suggests that perhaps instead we should see only the confusion, inconsistency, forgetfulness, and contrariety of a sick man cut off from his familiar milieu and his customary access to politics in the party and events in the country.[29] Sometimes, in his final months, Lenin would propose something in the evening and then, forgetting it entirely, something else the next morning. In this light, his attack on bureaucracy and careerism may indicate only desperation and inconsistency. For several years, he had warned of "communist arrogance," by which he meant the attitude of officials who tried to solve all problems by administrative methods and orders from above. Now, perhaps in confusion, he suggested a rash of bureaucratic reforms, none of which was likely to mitigate the ills of one-party rule. Several times, he suggested doubling or tripling the size of the Central Committee by adding fifty or a hundred ordinary workers. He also proposed correcting the ills of bureaucracy by merging or expanding existing bureaucratic institutions. Tragically, he did

Figure 5. *Lenin and Stalin in the Garden at Gorki, March 1923*
Despite their stormy relationship, Stalin continued to visit Lenin until the former leader lost the ability to communicate. This picture was presumably taken to demonstrate their close friendship. That very month, Lenin threatened to break off all relations with Stalin if Stalin did not apologize for insulting Krupskaia, Lenin's wife.

not see, or was not willing to see, that the bureaucratic ills he so detested or pretended to detest—arbitrariness, bribery, mismanagement—stemmed chiefly from one-party rule and from the absence of any legal countervailing force to the dictatorial power he himself had created. Moreover, in casting about for new solutions, the failing leader (in fact, the former leader) may not have realized that no one in the party elite intended to take his proposals seriously.

Lenin suffered another massive stroke on March 10, 1923. During the last ten months of his life, he was unable to speak, read, or write. He died on January 21, 1924, just short of his fifty-fourth birthday (see Figure 6).

21 января 1924 года в Горках, под Москвой, умер Ленин — вождь и основатель партии большевиков, вождь трудящихся всего мира. Знамя Ленина, знамя партии высоко поднял и понес дальше Сталин — выдающийся ученик Ленина, лучший сын большевистской партии, достойный преемник и великий продолжатель дела Ленина

В. И. Ленин в гробу

Figure 6.   Pravda's *Coverage of Lenin's Funeral Service, 1924*

Stalin organized Lenin's funeral. The Politburo disregarded Krupskaia's pleas and ordered Lenin embalmed and displayed in a mausoleum in front of the Kremlin. Among the eulogies, Stalin's was later remembered for his sworn oaths to the deceased, which ended with a promise to work for the Communist International. Lenin remains on display in 2006 despite protests from democratic politicians.
Pravda, January 28, 1924.

LENIN'S LEGACY

Lenin's legacy, above all, was the Soviet system. Why then is it important to read what he wrote? The answer is that he could hardly have acted as he did or gained the support that he did without formulating and propagating his thoughts in writing. Reading the following documents, we can evaluate Lenin's actions in their proper context and understand how he gained the power to rule Russia and what that power meant in practice.

Lenin figures in the history of tsarist Russia, the revolutionary movement, World War I, the Russian Civil War, the development of the Soviet Union, and the history of Europe after World War I. The question arises as to whether he was a product of his environment and his era or a unique historical actor who broke with the past to shape the future. From one vantage point, his efforts to reconstitute the Russian state as a great power after the February Revolution seem almost inevitable, since the threat posed to Russia by the advanced imperial nations of Western Europe may have led Russians to search for such a strong, nationalist-minded leader.[30] Yet the October Revolution can also be seen as an untimely interruption in Russia's progress to democracy and a market economy. Historians are right to ask whether, without Lenin, his followers would have seized power on their own.

A related question concerns Lenin's relationship with power. He modified Marxism by imagining a proletarian revolution in which revolutionaries would use the state to create a new social order. But this innovation fails to shed light on a broader question: Did Lenin seek power for its own ends, as a nationalist seeking a powerful Russia, or as an ideologue intent on an ideal society? The documents provide instances consistent with each interpretation. For example, Lenin already appears as a nationalist arguing for a centralized state system without much regional autonomy in his "Resolution on the National Question" (Document 8, May 1917). A few months later, however, he sounds like the most optimistic utopian in "The Impending Catastrophe and How to Combat It" (Document 11, September 1917), in which he describes the ease of constructing a new state system. And, two months after that, power and control seem to be his chief concerns when he justifies the need for an all-Bolshevik government (Document 14).

Lenin was a great innovator. He was not the only Russian revolutionary to advocate an elite party, but he alone created one. He was also the first Russian revolutionary to link war and revolution (see Document 4). Was Lenin, then, more of an innovator than a Marxist?

A number of documents reveal his fidelity to the most fundamental Marxist concepts, such as the stages of history and inevitability of class conflict. Again and again in his writings, Lenin blames "class enemies" for sabotage and other crimes, as he does in a telegram from 1918 (Document 24). Yet Lenin also adjusted Marx's negative categorization of the peasantry to suit Russia as a peasant country and described his revolution as a revolution of workers and peasants (Document 9). Lenin allowed for class war in Russian villages between rich and poor peasants and even described the Soviet state as a "dictatorship of the proletariat and the poor peasantry" (Document 14).

The issue of Lenin's pragmatism or dogmatism also arises with respect to the New Economic Policy and the policy initiatives that he promoted in the last months of his life. In the case of the NEP, the question is simple. Was he willing to change direction decisively in the face of economic collapse and rebellion, or did he compromise unwillingly, always yearning for the moment when he could return to the ideologically purer policies of greater state control? The documents related to the Tenth Party Congress tell the story of his decisive change in policy, but also of his unwillingness to accept the NEP as final. Readers will need to decide for themselves how to balance Lenin's willingness to open up the rural economy with his urge to control economic life.

A final issue concerns Lenin's last months. Do his writings in this final phase constitute a rethinking of his entire program and an attempt to redirect the party and society on more pluralistic lines, or was he simply reaching again for bureaucratic solutions as his physical and mental powers failed? The documents provide much to think about on this issue.

Our final word of introduction concerns Lenin in history. Lenin has not provoked the ongoing debates and discussions that flourish among historians of Stalin; he has been fortunate in his biographers and has been treated in a comparatively balanced manner in contemporary historical literature. Historians now largely agree that although the Bolsheviks' seizure of power in 1917 and the socialist revolution under Lenin's leadership set the course for Stalin's dictatorial regime, Stalin's rule was not the predestined result of Lenin's.[31]

In recent studies, some historians have stressed the weakness of civil society in Imperial Russia and, therefore, the ease and near-inevitability of the Bolsheviks' seizure of power.[32] Others have stressed the vitality of Imperial Russia.[33] Still others have found continuities between late imperial culture and Bolshevism or cited the Bolsheviks' appeal to those seeking social and political change.[34] From one perspective, Lenin addressed a range of dilemmas from economic backwardness to social disorder; from another, he simply seized a moment to make history. There is much to be learned from each of these lines of research, and such arguments will persist as long as Russian history is studied. Lenin's political effectiveness in accomplishing his goals is undeniable; the extent to which that effectiveness served a heartfelt devotion to a Marxist worldview, an ambitious desire for untrammeled power, or a combination of the two undoubtedly remains a matter of debate.

NOTES

[1] Until February 1918, Russians used the Julian calendar, which was twelve days behind the Gregorian in the nineteenth century and thirteen days behind in the twentieth. Hence the February Revolution actually took place in March according to our dating. New style dates are given in parentheses when appropriate.

[2] *Istoricheskii Arhiv*, no. 1 (1992); 216. This figure was given by the director of the Marxism-Leninism Institute of the Central Committee of the Communist Party of the Soviet Union, G L. Smirnov, in a note to the CC of the CPSU.

[3] Robert C. Allen, *Farm to Factory: A Reinterpretation of the Soviet Industrial Revolution* (Princeton, N.J.: Princeton University Press, 2003), 1–6.

[4] Allen, *Farm to Factory*, 25.

[5] A. G. Rashin, *Naselenie Rossiii za 100 Let (1811–1913): Statisticheskie ocherki*, ed. S. G. Strumilin (Moscow: Gos. statisticheskoe izdatel'stvo, 1956), 90.

[6] B. N. Mironov, *Sotsial'naia istoriia Rossii. Period imperii (XVIII–nachalo XX v.)* vol. 2 (Moscow: Dmitrii Bulanin, 1999), tables 10 and 11, 387–88.

[7] Mironov, *Sotsial'naia istoriia Rossii*, vol. 1, 139.

[8] David Mitch, "Education and Skill of the British Labor Force," in *The Cambridge Economic History of Modern Britain*, vol. 1 (Cambridge: Cambridge University Press, 2004), 351.

[9] Rashin, *Naselenie Rossii za 100 Let*, 304.

[10] Ibid., 299.

[11] Optimists include Paul Gregory, *Before Command: An Economic History of Russia from Emancipation to the First Five Year-Plan* (Princeton, N.J.: Princeton University Press, 1994); Boris Mironov, *The Social History of Imperial Russia* (Boulder, Colo.: Westview Press, 2000); and Peter Gatrell, *The Tsarist Economy: 1850–1917* (New York: St. Martin's Press, 1986). Pessimists include Thomas Owen, *Russian Corporate Capitalism from Peter the Great to Perestroika* (Oxford: Oxford University Press, 1995); and Allen, *Farm to Factory*.

[12] Soviet ethnographers charted these changes in *Russkie; Istoriko-etnograficheskii atlas "Russkie"* (Moscow: Nauka, 1963).

[13] V. I. Lenin, *Neizvestnye Dokumenty 1891–1922* (Moscow: ROSSPEN, 1999), 51–53; Boris I. Nicolaevsky, *Tainye Stranitsy Istorii* (Moscow: Izdatel'stvo gumanitarnoi Literatury, 1995), 11–92.

[14]Alexander Rabinovich, *The Bolsheviks Come to Power* (New York: Norton, 1976); Diane Koenker, *Moscow Workers and the 1917 Revolution* (Princeton, N.J.: Princeton University Press, 1981).

[15]"XI S'ezd R.K.P. Utrennie Zasedanie 28–9 Marta, Zakliuchitel'noe slovo tov. Lenina," *Pravda*, March 30, 1922, 1.

[16]Orlando Figes and Boris Kolonitsky, *Interpreting the Russian Revolution: The Language and Symbols of 1917* (New Haven, Conn.: Yale University Press, 1999), 153–91; and B. I. Kolonitskii, *Simvoly vlasti i bor'ba za vlast'* (St. Petersburg: RAN, 2001), particularly part II.

[17]V. I. Lenin, *Collected Works*, vol. 27 (Moscow: Progress Publishers, 1965), 92–93.

[18]Richard Pipes argues in *Russia under the Bolshevik Regime* (New York: Vintage, 1995), 9–14, that the Bolsheviks' advantages in addition to unity included superior resources and possession of the heart of the country.

[19]Lenin, *Collected Works*, vol. 29, 163.

[20]Ibid., vol. 30, 487.

[21]Ibid.

[22]Ibid., vol. 33, 330–34.

[23]Ibid., vol. 33, 280.

[24]Jane Burbank, *Intelligentsia and Revolution: Russian Views of Bolshevism 1917–1922* (New York and Oxford: Oxford University Press, 1986), 49.

[25]Lenin, *Collected Works*, vol. 33, 480. Moshe Lewin wrote: "[Lenin's] 'superstructure' came before the 'base.' The former was supposedly socialist, but suspended temporarily in a kind of vacuum, and the problem consisted not, as it was hoped, in adapting the recalcitrant 'superstructure' to the 'basis,' but in the first creating and then lifting up the 'basis' to the lofty heights of the most advanced political 'superstructure.' " The author added, "It might have looked ridiculous that the roof should shape the foundation and not vice versa." Quotes from Moshe Levin, "The Social Background of Stalinism," in *Stalinism: Essays in Historical Interpretation*, Robert C. Tucker ed. (New York: Norton, 1977), 113, 114.

[26]*Pravda*, June 19, 1924.

[27]Terry Martin, *The Affirmative Action Empire: Nations and Nationalism in the Soviet Union, 1923–1939* (Ithaca, N.Y.: Cornell University Press, 2001), 13–14.

[28]See, for example, Beryll Williams, *Lenin* (Harlow, England: Longman, 2001), 191–97.

[29]Lenin, *Collected Works*, vol. 33, 465. The term *Lenin's political testament* was coined by N. I. Bukharin, who was trying with A. I. Rykov and some other party-state leaders to stop Stalin's turn to extraordinary measures. Bukharin published his article "Lenin's Political Testament" in *Pravda* on January 24, 1929. From Stephen Cohen, *Bukharin and the Bolshevik Revolution: A Political Biography. 1888–1938* (Oxford: Oxford University Press, 1988), 393–94.

[30]This was the classic argument of Theodore Von Laue in *Why Lenin? Why Stalin?* (Philadelphia: Lippincott, 1964).

[31]See, for example, essays by R. Tucker, S. Kohen, and other authors in *Stalinism: Essays in Historical Interpretation* and the essays by Robert Service and Felix Patrikeeff in *Redefining Stalinism*, ed. Harold Shukman (London: Frank Cass, 2003).

[32]Moshe Lewin, *The Making of the Soviet System* (New York: Pantheon Books, 1995).

[33]See, for example, Jeffrey Brooks, *When Russia Learned to Read: Literacy and Popular Literature, 1861–1917* (Evanston, Ill.: Northwestern University Press, 2003, 1985); Louise McReynolds, *The News under Russia's Old Regime: The Development of a Mass-Circulation Press* (Princeton, N.J.: Princeton University Press, 1991); Mark D. Steinberg, *Proletarian Imagination: Self, Modernity, and the Sacred in Russia, 1910–1925* (Ithaca, N.Y.: Cornell University Press, 2002); Sergei Zhuk, *Russia's Lost Reformation: Peasants, Millennialism and Radical Sects in Southern Russia and Ukraine,*

1830–1917 (Baltimore: Johns Hopkins University and Woodrow Wilson Center Press, 2004).

[34]See, for example, Figes and Kolonitsky, *Interpreting the Russian Revolution*, Kolonitskii, *Simvoly vlasti*; and Peter Holquist, *Making War: Forging Revolution* (Cambridge, Mass.: Harvard University Press, 2002).

PART TWO

The Documents

1

Lenin and the Bolshevik Seizure of Power, 1900–1917

The years 1900 to 1917 were triumphant for Lenin. He returned from Siberian exile in 1900 at the age of 30, settled briefly in European Russia, and then left for Western Europe. He came back seventeen years later in April 1917 as a famous revolutionary and the leader of a militant party. While abroad, he had helped create that party, attracting followers both inside and outside of Russia. Once in Russia again, he planned for the seizure of power of which he had long dreamed.

Lenin's writings prior to the October Revolution are notable for his preoccupation with appropriate tactics for making a revolution and for the innovations he made to Marxist theory. Most notably, Lenin believed that peasant Russia was ripe for revolution despite Marx's argument that a developed bourgeois society must precede a proletarian one. Readers of Lenin's "April Theses" (Document 6) and the other selections in this chapter can identify several constants in his prerevolutionary thought, including hostility to bourgeois life and practices, unwavering interest in acquiring and employing state power for revolutionary ends, and impatience for the revolution to begin. In 1902, in *What Is to Be Done?* (Document 2), Lenin explained how to make a revolution in a backward society with a "party of a new type," that is, an elite centralized party that could seize power and also rule. The Revolution of 1905 and the effects of World War I (1914–1918) on the great bourgeois nations convinced him that an opportunity for European revolution unforeseen by Marx and Engels had arisen.

The documents in this chapter also illuminate Lenin's struggle for power. In almost every one, Lenin the pragmatist wrestles with Lenin the ideologue. Believing that he alone knew how to take power, however, Lenin was always innovating and modifying the teachings of Marx and Engels. Where then does the balance rest between his flexibility and his commitment to Marxism in his theoretical writings and his tactical directives?

Lenin as a Theorist of Revolution

1

From *The Urgent Tasks of Our Movement*
December 1900

*The following excerpt reveals the logic of Lenin's early belief in the immi-
nence of revolution. Many of his fellow Marxists were drawn to the workers' struggle for improved working conditions and better wages, but
Lenin had a more radical vision. In that respect, this essay is pivotal to
his thought. Why, if he sought a proletarian revolution, did Lenin refuse
to identify himself with the workers' struggle for a better life? Why did he
believe that incremental victories that improved workers' lives were no
victories at all?*

Our principal and fundamental task is to facilitate the political development and the political organization of the working class. Those who
push this task into the background, who refuse to subordinate to it all
the special tasks and particular methods of struggle, are following a
false path and causing serious harm to the movement. And it is being
pushed into the background, firstly, by those who call upon revolutionaries to employ only the forces of isolated conspiratorial circles cut off
from the working-class movement in the struggle against the government. It is being pushed into the background, secondly, by those who
restrict the content and scope of political propaganda, agitation, and
organization; who think it fit and proper to treat the workers to "politics" only at exceptional moments in their lives, only on festive occa-
sions; who too solicitously substitute demands for partial concessions
from the autocracy for the political struggle against the autocracy; and
who do not go to sufficient lengths to ensure that these demands for
partial concessions are raised to the status of a systematic, implacable
struggle of a revolutionary, working-class party against the autocracy.

V. I. Lenin, *Collected Works*, vol. 4 (Moscow: Foreign Languages Publishing House,
1960), 369.

2

From *What Is to Be Done?*

1902

This essay represents Lenin's most important contribution to revolutionary practice. In 1900, he and others established the Marxist newspaper Iskra *(The Spark), which Lenin cast as the ideological center of a new party. Yet it was an outlet journal for educated activists, and was much too difficult for rank-and-file proletarians to understand. In that respect,* Iskra *suited Lenin's idea of an elite revolutionary party, which he describes in the following selection. Lenin took his title from the well-known novel of the same name by mid-nineteenth-century revolutionary Nicholai Chernyshevsky (1828–1889), who imagined an ascetic revolutionary hero and an ideal community. The occasion for Lenin's essay was the struggle for leadership that occurred within the Russian Social-Democratic Workers' Party before the Second Party Congress (1903), at which the split between Lenin's Bolsheviks and the Mensheviks took place. Whereas the Mensheviks tended to support a broad party organization in which ordinary workers and trade unionists could participate on a part-time basis, Lenin wanted a centralized underground party of professional revolutionaries that could more easily avoid the police. He believed that workers needed such a party because they were unable to develop revolutionary ideology and tactics on their own. Lenin drove home this message by contrasting the aimless and ineffective "spontaneity" of the masses with the purposeful "consciousness" of the Social-Democrats, his revolutionary elite. Thus he distinguishes between a mass party of "a hundred fools" and an elite party that he characterizes as "a dozen wise men." In considering this document, readers should note Lenin's use of the pronoun "we" and his image of a group of militant devotees marching along a single path.*

We are marching in a compact group along a precipitous and difficult path, firmly holding each other by the hand. We are surrounded on all sides by enemies, and we have to advance almost constantly under

V. I. Lenin, *Collected Works*, vol. 5 (Moscow: Progress Publishers, 1961), 355, 369–70, 374–75, 384, 460, 464.

their fire. We have combined, by a freely adopted decision, for the purpose of fighting the enemy, and not of retreating into the neighboring marsh, the inhabitants of which, from the very outset, have reproached us with having separated ourselves into an exclusive group and with having chosen the path of struggle instead of the path of conciliation. And now some among us begin to cry out: Let us go into the marsh! And when we begin to shame them, they retort: What backward people you are! Are you not ashamed to deny us the liberty to invite you to take a better road! Oh, yes, gentlemen! You are free not only to invite us, but to go yourselves wherever you will, even into the marsh. In fact, we think that the marsh is your proper place, and we are prepared to render *you* every assistance to get there. Only let go of our hands, don't clutch at us and don't besmirch the grand word freedom, for we too are "free" to go where we please, free to fight not only against the marsh, but also against those who are turning towards the marsh! . . .

Without revolutionary theory there can be no revolutionary movement. . . . [F]or Russian Social-Democrats the importance of theory is enhanced by three other circumstances, which are often forgotten: first, by the fact that our Party is only in the process of formation, its features are only just becoming defined, and it has as yet far from settled accounts with the other trends of revolutionary thought that threaten to divert the movement from the correct path. . . .

We shall have occasion further on to deal with the political and organizational duties which the task of emancipating the whole people from the yoke of autocracy imposes upon us. At this point, we wish to state only that the *role of vanguard fighter can be fulfilled only by a party that is guided by the most advanced theory.* . . .

In the previous chapter we pointed out how *universally* absorbed the educated youth of Russia was in the theories of Marxism in the middle of the nineties. In the same period the strikes that followed the famous St. Petersburg industrial war of 1896[1] assumed a similar general character. Their spread over the whole of Russia clearly showed the depth of the newly awakening popular movement, and if we are to speak of the "spontaneous element" then, of course, it is this strike movement which, first and foremost, must be regarded as spontaneous. But there is spontaneity and spontaneity. Strikes occurred in

---

[1] Lenin refers to widespread strikes provoked in part by the St. Petersburg factory owners' refusal to pay workers for the three days of celebrations on the occasion of the coronation of the new tsar, Nicholas II.

Russia in the seventies and sixties (and even in the first half of the nineteenth century), and they were accompanied by the "spontaneous" destruction of machinery, etc. Compared with these "revolts," the strikes of the nineties might even be described as "conscious," to such an extent do they mark the progress which the working-class movement made in that period. This shows that the "spontaneous element," in essence, represents nothing more nor less than consciousness in an *embryonic form*. Even the primitive revolts expressed the awakening of consciousness to a certain extent. The workers were losing their age-long faith in the permanence of the system which oppressed them and began . . . [ellipses in the original] I shall not say to understand, but to sense the necessity for collective resistance, definitely abandoning their slavish submission to the authorities. But this was, nevertheless, more in the nature of outbursts of desperation and vengeance than of *struggle*. . . . Taken by themselves, these strikes were simply trade union struggles, not yet Social-Democratic struggles. They marked the awakening antagonisms between workers and employers; but the workers were not, and could not be, conscious of the irreconcilable antagonism of their interests to the whole of the modern political and social system, i.e., theirs was not yet Social-Democratic consciousness. In this sense, the strikes of the nineties, despite the enormous progress they represented as compared with the "revolts," remained a purely spontaneous movement.

We have said that *there could not have been* Social-Democratic consciousness among the workers. It would have to be brought to them from without. The history of all countries shows that the working class, exclusively by its own effort, is able to develop only trade-union consciousness, i.e., the conviction that it is necessary to combine in unions, fight the employers, and strive to compel the government to pass necessary labor legislation, etc.[2] The theory of socialism, however, grew out of the philosophic, historical, and economic theories elaborated by educated representatives of the propertied classes, by intellectuals. . . .

Since there can be no talk of an independent ideology formulated by the working masses themselves in the process of their movement,[3]

---

[2]Trade Unionism does not exclude "politics" altogether, as some imagine. Trade unions have always conducted some political (but not Social-Democratic) agitation and struggle. . . . [This note appears in the original text.]

[3]This does not mean, of course, that the workers have no part in creating such an ideology. Lenin had great hopes for educated workers.

the *only* choice is—either bourgeois or socialist ideology. There is no middle course (for mankind has not created a "third" ideology, and, moreover, in a society torn by class antagonisms there can never be a non-class or an above-class ideology). Hence, to belittle the socialist ideology *in any way, to turn aside from it in the slightest degree* means to strengthen bourgeois ideology. . . .

The moral to be drawn from this is simple. If we begin with the solid foundation of a strong organization of revolutionaries, we can ensure the stability of the movement as a whole and carry out the aims both of Social-Democracy and of trade unions proper. . . .

I assert that it is far more difficult to unearth a dozen wise men than a hundred fools. . . . As I have stated repeatedly, by "wise men," in connection with organization, I mean *professional revolutionaries*, irrespective of whether they have developed from among students or working men. I assert: (1) that no revolutionary movement can endure without a stable organization of leaders maintaining continuity; (2) that the broader the popular mass drawn spontaneously into the struggle, which forms the basis of the movement and participates in it, the more urgent the need for such an organization, and the more solid this organization must be (for it is much easier for all sorts of demagogues to side-track the more backward sections of the masses); (3) that such an organization must consist chiefly of people professionally engaged in revolutionary activity.

3

From *The Party Organization and Party Literature*
November 1905

After 1905, Lenin confronted a new situation: The tsar, Nicholas II, had instituted a partial freedom of the press in response to the threat of revolution. Prepublication censorship of newspapers was discontinued, although publishers were frequently fined and periodicals were often closed for criticizing the autocracy. Lenin reacted to this new circumstance in November 1905 by demanding that all party publications be

V. I. Lenin, *Collected Works*, vol. 10 (Moscow: Progress Publishers, 1967), 45, 47–48.

subordinated to party control to ensure a unified message and a correct ideological stance. When he wrote this essay, Lenin had publications and writers affiliated with the party in mind, but once in power he did in fact seek to oversee and control all public speech. In the essay, he observes that it is not good enough for writers of party publications to produce articles that are "nine-tenths party literature," that is, almost completely reflective of party directives. Rather, he demands that articles be in complete accordance with party ideology. Note Lenin's observation in the following essay that there can be no "non-class" literature or art since all such works reflect the views and interests of one class or another. Later, Soviet cultural authorities used this article to justify the repression of discordant writers and other cultural figures. Should historians consider this when reading this text, as some have done, or ignore it?

Today literature, even that published "legally," can be nine-tenths party literature. It must become party literature. In contradistinction to bourgeois customs, to the profit-making, commercialized bourgeois press, to bourgeois literary careerism and individualism, "aristocratic anarchism" and drive for profit, the socialist proletariat must put forward the principle of *party literature*, must develop this principle and put it into practice as fully and completely as possible.

What is this principle of party literature? It is not simply that, for the socialist proletariat, literature cannot be a means of enriching individuals or groups: it cannot, in fact, be an individual undertaking, independent of the common cause of the proletariat. Down with non-partisan writers! Down with literary supermen! Literature must become *part* of the common cause of the proletariat, "a cog and a screw" of one single great Social-Democratic mechanism set in motion by the entire politically-conscious vanguard of the entire working class. Literature must become a component of organized, planned and integrated Social-Democratic Party work. . . .

We want to establish, and we shall establish, a free press, free not simply from the police, but also from capital, from careerism, and what is more, free from bourgeois-anarchist individualism. . . .

There can be no real and effective "freedom" in a society based on the power of money, in a society in which the masses of working people live in poverty and the handful of rich live like parasites. . . . The freedom of the bourgeois writer, artist or actress is simply masked (or hypocritically masked) dependence on the money-bag, on corruption, on prostitution.

And we socialists expose this hypocrisy and rip off the false labels, not in order to arrive at a non-class literature and art (that will be possible only in a socialist classless[4] society), but to contrast this hypocritically free literature, which is in reality linked to the bourgeoisie, with a really free one that will be *openly* linked to the proletariat.

4

From *Imperialism, the Highest Stage of Capitalism*

1916

Lenin strengthened his reputation as a theorist among party members with Imperialism, The Highest State of Capitalism, *which he wrote in early 1916 in Switzerland. He drew heavily on the work of the British economist J. A. Hobson, who linked capitalism to empire in his* Imperialism *(1902). Lenin's study is notable for its emphasis on the changing character of imperialism, from colonies to economic domination, and for its argument that imperialism was the final phase of capitalism, a final division of the world among capitalist nations that would lead to war. This was an important departure from Marx and Engels, neither of whom allowed for such a stage in the development of capitalism or for the importance of war as the midwife of revolution.*

The principal feature of the latest stage of capitalism is the domination of monopolist associations of big employers. These monopolies are most firstly established when *all* the sources of raw materials are captured by one group, and we have seen with what zeal the international capitalist associations exert every effort to deprive their rivals of all opportunity of competing, to buy up, for example, ironfields, oilfields,

---

[4]The official English text is "extraclass." This is a mistranslation of the Russian *vneklassovoe obshchestvo* and hence our correction.

V. I. Lenin, *Collected Works*, vol. 22 (Moscow: Progress Publishers, 1964), 260, 266, 275–76.

etc. Colonial possession alone gives the monopolies complete guarantee against all contingencies in the struggle against competitors, including the case of the adversary wanting to be protected by a law establishing a state monopoly. The more capitalism is developed, the more strongly the shortage of raw materials is felt, the more intense the competition and the hunt for sources of raw materials throughout the whole world, the more desperate the struggle for the acquisition of colonies. . . .

If it were necessary to give the briefest possible definition of imperialism we should have to say that imperialism is the monopoly stage of capitalism. Such a definition would include what is most important, for, on the one hand, finance capital is the bank capital of a few very big monopolist banks, merged with the capital of the monopolist associations of industrialists; and, on the other hand, the division of the world is the transition from a colonial policy which has extended without hindrance to territories unseized by any capitalist power, to a colonial policy of monopolist possession of the territory of the world, which has been completely divided up. . . .

The question is: what means other than war could there be *under capitalism* to overcome the disparity between the development of productive forces and the accumulation of capital on the one side, and the division of colonies and spheres of influence for finance capital on the other?

5

From *The State and Revolution*

1917

In The State and Revolution, *Lenin emphasizes the role of the state in society both before and after the proletarian revolution. Filled with enthusiasm for the future revolution, he finished this work in the summer of 1917, after returning to Russia from Switzerland. It appeared in August, several months before the Bolsheviks seized power under Lenin's*

V. I. Lenin, *Collected Works*, vol. 25 (Moscow: Progress Publishers, 1964), 387, 396, 404, 413, 420–21, 425–27, 455–56.

leadership. The text is a mix of vague theorizing and precise data, much like Imperialism *(Document 4).* The State and Revolution *illuminates Lenin's view of the state as a weapon of class struggle and a tool to transform society. In contrast to Engels's suggestion that the state "withers away" once the proletariat gains power, Lenin stresses the lasting need for the state. In this work, Lenin describes a system of government much more open than the one that he would help to create. He also supposes a smooth transition from a bourgeois economy to a proletarian one. Both for its idyllic qualities and its celebration of the state as an instrument of social transformation, this proved to be one of Lenin's most popular and accessible works. He does not discuss the elite vanguard party that he idealized at length in other writings, but he allows for the party's power and rejects the parliamentary system as bourgeois. He also envisions the victorious proletariat's use of the state to crush their enemies.*

The state is a product and a manifestation of the *irreconcilability* of class antagonisms. The state arises where, when and insofar as class antagonisms objectively *cannot* be reconciled. And, conversely, the existence of the state proves that class antagonisms are irreconcilable. . . .

It is safe to say that of this argument of Engels's, which is so remarkably rich in ideas, only one point has become an integral part of socialist thought among modern socialist parties, namely, that according to Marx the state "withers away"—as distinct from the anarchist doctrine of the "abolition" of the state. . . .

Such an "interpretation," however, is the crudest distortion of Marxism, advantageous only to the bourgeoisie. . . .

The proletariat needs state power, a centralized organization of force, an organization of violence, both to crush the resistance of the exploiters and to *lead* the enormous mass of the population—the peasants, the petty bourgeoisie, and semi-proletarians—in the work of organising a socialist economy.

By educating the workers' party, Marxism educates the vanguard of the proletariat, capable of assuming power and *leading the whole people* to socialism, of directing and organizing the new system, of being the teacher, the guide, the leader of all the working and exploited people in organizing their social life without the bourgeoisie and against the bourgeoisie. . . .

The essence of Marx's theory of the state has been mastered only by those who realize that the dictatorship of a *single* class is necessary not only for every class society in general, not only for the *proletariat* which has overthrown the bourgeoisie, but also for the entire *historical period* which separates capitalism from "classless society," from communism. . . .

***

Capitalist culture has *created* large-scale production, factories, railways, the postal service, telephones, etc., and *on this basis* the great majority of the functions of the old "state power" have become so simplified and can be reduced to such exceedingly simple operations of registration, filing and checking that they can be easily performed by every literate person, can quite easily be performed for ordinary "workmen's wages," and that these functions can (and must) be stripped of every shadow of privilege, of every semblance of "official grandeur."

All officials, without exception, elected and subject to recall *at any time*, their salaries reduced to the level of ordinary "workmen's wages"—these simply and "self-evident" democratic measures, while completely uniting the interests of the workers and the majority of the peasants, at the same time serve as a bridge leading from capitalism to socialism. . . .

Capitalism simplifies the functions of "state" administration; it makes it possible to cast "bossing" aside and to confine the whole matter to the organization of the proletarians (as the ruling class), which will hire "workers, foremen and accountants" in the name of the whole of society.

We are not utopians, we do not "dream" of dispensing *at once* with all administration, with all subordination. These anarchist dreams, based upon incomprehension of the tasks of the proletarian dictatorship, are totally alien to Marxism, and, as a matter of fact, serve only to postpone the socialist revolution until people are different. No, we want the socialist revolution with people as they are now, with people who cannot dispense with subordination, control and "foremen and accountants."

The subordination, however, must be to the armed vanguard of all the exploited and working people, i.e., to the proletariat. . . .

We, the workers, shall organize large-scale production on the basis of what capitalism has already created, relying on our own experience as workers, we shall establish strict, iron discipline supported by the state power of the armed workers. We shall reduce the role of the state officials to that of simply carrying out our instructions as responsible, revocable, moderately paid "foremen and accountants" (of course, with the aid of technicians of all sorts, types and degrees). . . .

To organize the *whole* economy on the lines of the postal service so that the technicians, foremen and accountants, as well as *all* officials, shall receive salaries no higher than "a workmen's wage," all under the control and leadership of the armed proletariat—this is our immediate aim. This is the state and this is the economic foundation we need. This is what will bring about the abolition of parliamentarism and the preservation of representative institutions. This is what will rid the laboring classes of the bourgeoisie's prostitution of these institutions. . . .

In the usual arguments about the state, the mistake is constantly made against which Engels warned and which we have in passing indicated above, namely, it is constantly forgotten that the abolition of the state means also the abolition of democracy: that the withering away of the state means the withering away of democracy.

At first sight this assertion seems exceedingly strange and incomprehensible; indeed, someone may even begin to suspect us of expecting the advent of a system of society in which the principle of subordination of the minority to the majority will not be observed — for democracy means the recognition of this very principle.

No, democracy is *not* identical with the subordination of the minority to the majority. Democracy is a *state* which recognizes the subordination of the minority to the majority, i.e., an organization for the systematic use of *force* by one class against another, by one section of the population against another.

We set ourselves the ultimate aim of abolishing the state, i.e., all organized and systematic violence, all use of violence against people in general. We do not expect the advent of a system of society in which the principle of subordination of the minority to the majority will not be observed. In striving for socialism, however, we are convinced that it will develop into communism and, therefore, that the need for violence against people in general, for the *subordination* of one man to another, and of one section of the population to another, will vanish altogether since people will *become accustomed* to observing the elementary conditions of social life *without violence* and *without subordination*.

The Path to the Bolsheviks' Seizure of Power

The documents in this section concern two issues: gaining power and winning support. The six months between Lenin's return to Petrograd in April, soon after the February Revolution of 1917 and his seizure of power witnessed the Provisional Government's unsuccessful struggle to manage the war, the economy, and widespread discontent. Perhaps the Provisional Government's most fateful decision was to remain loyal to its British and French allies and continue the unpopular war against the Central Powers (Germany, Austria-Hungary, Bulgaria, and Turkey).

Lenin took the party by storm upon his return to Petrograd with his call for proletarian revolution and promise of power in his "April Theses" (Document 6). He appealed to ordinary workers, soldiers, and peasants by promising stability, workers' control over factories, land, and peace (Document 9). He offered the nationalities the right to self-determination and succession despite his belief that they should remain part of revolutionary Russia (Document 8). These were promises that he could hardly keep, and Lenin, as a realistic politician, no doubt understood this. Yet Lenin's promises served the Bolsheviks well in gaining popular support. At the same time, Lenin's speeches and writings built up the party during this period by attracting new members, including the semi-educated people of common origins who became local leaders. Most of all, the "April Theses" energized the Bolshevik elite who had been tentatively supporting a pro-war policy. Lenin denounced the war and the Provisional Government and appealed for a new socialist international to lead a worldwide anticapitalist struggle.[5]

6

From *The Tasks of the Proletariat in the Present Revolution (April Theses)*

April 1917

When Lenin arrived at the Finland Station in Petrograd in April 1917, he gave a speech condemning the Provisional Government and challenging Petrograd's Bolshevik leaders, who had tentatively supported the Provisional Government's pro-war policy. He published the notes for his speech

[5]The Second International (1889–1914), which replaced the First International-Working Men's Association (1864–1876) of Marx's era, had failed to oppose World War I and disintegrated.

V. I. Lenin, *Collected Works*, vol. 24 (Moscow: Progress Publishers, 1964), 21–24.

in Pravda. *To the shock and surprise of more timid colleagues, Lenin denounced the war and the Provisional Government and called for proletarian revolution and soviet rule, even though Bolsheviks lacked a majority in the soviets.*

1) ... not the slightest concession to "revolutionary defencism. ...

2) The specific feature of the present situation in Russia is that the country is *passing* from the first stage of the revolution—which, owing to the insufficient class-consciousness and organization of the proletariat, placed power in the hands of the bourgeoisie—to its *second* stage, which must place power in the hands of the proletariat and the poorest sections of the peasants. ...

3) No support for the Provisional Government. ...

4) ... As long as we are in the minority we carry on the work of criticizing and exposing errors and at the same time we preach the necessity of transferring the entire state power to the Soviets of Workers' Deputies, so that the people may overcome their mistakes by experience.

5) Not a parliamentary republic—to return to a parliamentary republic from the Soviets of Workers' Deputies would be a retrograde step—but a republic of Soviets of Workers', Agricultural Laborers' and Peasants' Deputies throughout the country, from top to bottom.
   Abolition of the police, the army and the bureaucracy.[6] ...

6) The weight of emphasis in the agrarian program to be shifted to the Soviets of Agricultural Laborers' Deputies.
   Confiscation of all landed estates.
   Nationalisation of *all* lands in the country, the land to be disposed of by the local Soviets of Agricultural Laborers' and Peasants' Deputies. ...

7) The immediate amalgamation of all banks in the country into a single national bank, and the institution of control over it by the Soviet of Workers' Deputies.

[6]Lenin meant for the standing army to be replaced by the arming of the whole people.

8) It is not our *immediate* task to "introduce" socialism, but only to bring social production and the distribution of products at once under the *control* of the Soviets of Workers' Deputies.

9) Party tasks:
    a) Immediate convocation of a Party congress;
    b) Alteration of the Party Programme. . . .

10) A new International. . . .

7

From *Speech in Favor of the Resolution on the War*
April 27 (May 10), 1917

Russia signed a secret treaty with Britain and France on August 23 (September 5), 1914, promising not to accept a separate peace and to agree on peace terms. Later secret agreements with the Allies promised Russia possession of Constantinople (Istanbul), the capital of Turkey, and control of the straits of the Black Sea that separate Constantinople from Europe. P. N. Miliukov, a former leader of the liberal Cadet Party and foreign minister in the Provisional Government, opposed accepting a peace agreement without these annexations and insisted that Russia continue to fight until victorious to realize these and other territorial gains. Socialists and leaders in the Soviets denounced Miliukov, and he was forced to resign in May 1917. Lenin condemned the secret treaties at the Seventh All-Russian Conference of the Russian Social Democratic Workers' Party (B) on May 10. The Bolsheviks would later publish these treaties, much to the consternation of the British and French. In the following document, Lenin advocates mass fraternization of Russian and German soldiers along the front to turn the world war into a revolutionary struggle and a civil war and rejects "revolutionary defencism," the moderate socialists' policy of supporting Russia's continuing participation in the war if the Germans would not agree to a peace without annexations.

V. I. Lenin, *Collected Works*, vol. 24 (Moscow: Progress Publishers, 1964), 259.

The people ought to be made aware that the present governments are carrying on the war on the basis of treaties concluded between the old governments. This, I feel, makes the contradictions between the capitalist interests and the will of the people stand out most strikingly, and it is for the propagandists to expose these contradictions, to draw the people's attention to them, to strive to explain them to the masses by appealing to their class-consciousness. The contents of these treaties leave no room for doubt that they promise enormous profits to the capitalists to be derived from robbing other countries. That is why they are always kept secret. There is not a republic in the world whose foreign policy is conducted in the open. It is fatuous, while the capitalist system exists, to expect the capitalists to open up their ledgers. While there is private ownership of the means of production, there is bound to be private ownership of shares and financial operations. The cornerstone of contemporary diplomacy is financial operations, which amount to robbing and strangling the weak nationalities. These, we believe, are the fundamental premises upon which evaluation of the war rests.

8

From *Resolution on the National Question*
May 1917

Although the Russian liberals had promised the non-Russian nationalities—the Finns, Poles, Ukrainians, Byelorussians, Georgians, Armenians, and others—various rights within the Empire and had won their support between 1905 and 1917, Lenin and the Bolsheviks went further in offering these nationalities the theoretical right to secede from the Empire, even though in practice they wished to keep them within revolutionary Russia. Lenin attributes national oppression to capitalism while qualifying the party's stand on independence in the following selection on the "national question" or the policy toward the non-Russian nationalities from the All-Russian Conference's "Resolution on the National Question." Movements among Russia's national minorities, including Poles, the Baltic peoples (Estonians, Latvians, and Lithuanians), Georgians, Finns, Ukrainians, and the Moslem population, had long pressed for

V. I. Lenin, *Collected Works*, vol. 24 (Moscow: Progress Publishers, 1964), 302–3.

more autonomy or outright independence. World War I emboldened them. Lenin sought the nationalities' support, and readers can decide whether his stance here is principled or simply devious.

The right of all the nations forming part of Russia freely to secede and form independent states must be recognized. To deny them this right, or to fail to take measures guaranteeing its practical realization, is equivalent to supporting a policy of seizure or annexation. Only the recognition by the proletariat of the right of nations to secede can ensure complete solidarity among the workers of the various nations and help to bring the nations closer together on truly democratic lines. . . .

The right of nations freely to secede must not be confused with the advisability of secession by a given nation at a given moment. The party of the proletariat must decide the latter question quite independently in each case, having regard to the interests of social development as a whole and the interests of the class struggle of the proletariat for socialism. . . .

The interests of the working class demand that workers of all nationalities in Russia should have common proletarian organizations: political, trade union, co-operative educational institutions, and so forth. Only the merging of the workers of the various nationalities into such common organizations will make it possible for the proletariat to wage a successful struggle against international Capital and bourgeois nationalism.

9

From *An Open Letter to the Delegates of the All-Russian Congress of Peasants' Deputies*

May 7 (29), 1917

When appealing to workers, peasants, and soldiers, Lenin stressed class issues, such as land for the peasants and workers' control of the factories, but he also promised broad democracy. In addition, he suggested that the Bolsheviks would resolve Russia's "crisis" and restore peace, order, and

V. I. Lenin, *Collected Works, vol.* 24 (Moscow: Progress Publishers, 1964), 370–74.

prosperity. This wide-ranging program helps explain the Bolsheviks' growing support among various segments of the lower classes from April through October, as well as their opponents' inability to rally the nation against the Bolsheviks once they had overthrown the Provisional Government.

The Bolsheviks adopted part of the agricultural program of the Socialist-Revolutionary Party by offering the peasants land. Yet the Bolsheviks urged the immediate seizure of the landowners' holdings, whereas the Provisional Government and the moderate socialists in the soviets wanted to resolve the issue in the framework of a new democratic constitution after the war. In the following open letter, Lenin promises the peasants land and contrasts the Bolsheviks' support for the seizure of land with the moderate socialists' decision to await a Constituent Assembly after the end of the war. He also expresses his conviction that the peasants would support the workers in a revolution. Without such support, his plan to seize power hardly made sense since as late as 1897 the rural population of European Russia constituted almost 90 percent of the whole, 93.4 million versus 12 million in cities.[7] Many peasant activists were literate and read aloud leaflets and broadsides such as the following to illiterate comrades.

All the land must belong to the people. All the landed estates must be turned over to the peasants without compensation. This is clear. The dispute here is whether or not the peasants in the local areas should take all the land at once, without paying any rent to the landowners, or wait until the Constituent Assembly meets.

Our Party believes that they should, and advises the peasants locally to take over all the land without delay, and to do it in as organized a way as possible, under no circumstances allowing damage to property and exerting every effort to increase the production of grain and meat since the troops at the front are in dire straights. In any case, although the final decision on how to dispose of the land will be made by the Constituent Assembly, a preliminary settlement now, at once, in time for the spring sowing, can be made only by local bodies, inasmuch as our Provisional Government, which is a government of

---

[7] A. G. Rashin, *Naselenie Rossii za 100 Let* (1811–1913), ed. S. G. Strumilin (Moscow: Gosudarstvennoe statisticheskoe izdatelstvo, 1956), 265.

the landowners and capitalists, is putting off the convocation of the Constituent Assembly and so far has not even fixed a date for it. . . .

Further. For all the land to pass over to the working people, a close alliance of the urban workers and the poor peasants (semi-proletarians) is essential. Unless such an alliance is formed, the capitalists cannot be defeated. And if they are not defeated, no transfer of the land to the people will deliver them from poverty. You cannot eat land, and without money, without capital, there is no way of obtaining implements, livestock, or seed. The peasants must trust not the capitalists or the rich muzhiks [peasants] (who are capitalists too), but only the urban workers. Only in alliance with the latter can the poor peasants ensure that the land, the railways, the banks, and the factories become the property of all the working people; if this is not done, the mere transfer of the land to the people cannot abolish want and pauperism. . . .

The second question is the question of the war.

This war is a war of conquest. It is being waged by the capitalists of all countries with predatory aims, to increase their profits. To the working people this war can spell only ruin, suffering, devastation, and brutalization. That is why our Party, the party of class-conscious workers and poor peasants, emphatically and unqualifiedly condemns this war, refuses to justify the capitalist of one country against the capitalist of another, refuses to support the capitalists of any country whatever, and is working for the speediest termination of the war through the overthrow of the capitalists in all countries, through a workers revolution in all countries. . . .

This brings me to the third and last of the questions I have mentioned: the question of state organization.

Russia must become a democratic republic. . . . The capitalists now have directed all their efforts at making the Russian republic as much like a monarchy as possible so that it might be changed back into a monarchy with the least difficulty (this has happened time and again in many countries). . . .

Our Party, the party of class-conscious workers and poor peasants, is therefore working for a democratic republic of another kind. We want a republic where there is no police that browbeats the people; where all officials, from the bottom up, are elective and displaceable whenever the people demand it, and are paid salaries not higher than the wages of a competent worker; where all army officers are similarly elective and where the standing army separated from the people and subordinated to classes alien to the people is replaced by the universally armed people, by a people's militia.

We want a republic where all state power, from the bottom up, belongs wholly and exclusively to the Soviets of Workers', Soldiers', Peasants', and other Deputies.

10

From *The Political Situation*

July 10 (23), 1917

In this document, Lenin describes a choice between a counterrevolutionary dictatorship and revolution. Kerensky was appointed president-minister in June while remaining minister of war and the navy. Discontent was boiling over. Peasants were seizing land, and the increasingly dictatorial Provisional Government tried but failed to prevent this from happening. In July, the government launched an ill-timed military offensive that caused numerous Russian casualties. At the beginning of the month, during the so-called July Days, armed workers and soldiers spontaneously filled the streets of Petrograd demanding all power to the soviets. Bolshevik leaders feared the reaction to a premature attempt to seize power but did not disown the demonstrators, many of whom carried banners with Bolshevik slogans. The moderate leaders of the Petrograd Soviet mobilized loyal regiments that faced down the demonstrators. The government then circulated documents purporting to show that the Germans were paying the Bolsheviks to hinder the war effort. Although the Bolsheviks did receive German money, Lenin used it for his own purposes, though the Germans may have believed they were getting their money's worth since Bolshevik antiwar propaganda led to desertions.[8] The accusation undercut the Bolsheviks' program and their standing. Lenin and a few other leaders fled Petrograd to avoid arrest. Despite this setback, Lenin's enthusiasm for revolution continued unabated. In this article from the July 10 issue of Pravda, *written when Lenin was in hiding, readers can sense his growing excitement.*

---

[8]Georgiy Chernyavskiy, *Pritchi O Pravde O Lzhi: Politicheskie Dramy Dvadtsatogo veka* (Kharkov: Oko, 2003), 24–36.

V. I. Lenin, *Collected Works*, vol. 25 (Moscow: Progress Publishers, 1964), 177–78.

All hopes for a peaceful development of the Russian revolution have vanished for good. This is the objective situation: either complete victory for the military dictatorship, or victory for the workers' armed uprising; the latter victory is only possible when the insurrection coincides with a deep, mass upheaval against the government and the bourgeoisie caused by economic disruption and the prolongation of the war.

The slogan "All Power to the Soviets!" was a slogan for peaceful development of the revolution which was possible in April, May, June, and up to July 5–9, i.e., up to the time when actual power passed into the hands of the military dictatorship. This slogan is no longer correct, for it does not take into account that power has changed hands and that the revolution has in fact been completely betrayed by the S.R.s and Mensheviks. . . . Let us gather forces, reorganize them, and resolutely prepare for the armed uprising, if the course of the crisis permits it on a really mass, country-wide scale. The transfer of land to the peasants is impossible at present without armed uprising, since the counter-revolutionaries, having taken power, have completely united with the landowners as a class.

The aim of the insurrection can only be to transfer power to the proletariat, supported by the poor peasants, with a view to putting our Party program into effect.

11

From *The Impending Catastrophe and How to Combat It*

September 10–14 (September 23–27), 1917

Throughout the summer, Lenin focused on gaining support not only from workers, but also from the peasants whom he identified with the petty bourgeoisie. He was also convinced that the revolution would spark a civil war, which perhaps became a self-fulfilling prophecy. As the Provisional Government continued to lose control, Lenin increasingly presented the Bolsheviks as the party of order and stability. In a pamphlet

V. I. Lenin, *Collected Works*, vol. 25 (Moscow: Progress Publishers, 1964), 323, 328–29.

written in September but published in late October, he offered a series of measures to prevent famine and economic dislocation.

Unavoidable catastrophe is threatening Russia. The railways are incredibly disorganized and the disorganization is progressing. The railways will come to a standstill. The delivery of raw materials and coal to the factories will cease. The delivery of grain will cease. The capitalists are deliberately and unremittingly sabotaging (damaging, stopping, disrupting, hampering) production, hoping that an unparalleled catastrophe will mean the collapse of the republic and democracy, and of the Soviets and proletarian and peasant associations generally, thus facilitating the return to a monarchy and the restoration of the unlimited power of the bourgeoisie and the landowners.

The danger of a great catastrophe and of famine is imminent. . . .

Six months of revolution have elapsed. The catastrophe is even closer. Unemployment has assumed a mass scale. . . .

We shall see that all a government would have had to do, if its name of revolutionary-democratic government were not merely a joke, would have been to decree, in the very first week of its existence, the adoption of the principal measures of control, to provide for strict and severe punishment to be meted out to capitalists who fraudulently evaded control, and to call upon the population itself to exercise supervision over the capitalists and see to it that they scrupulously observed the regulations on control—and control would have been introduced in Russia long ago.

These principal measures are:

(1) Amalgamation of all banks into a single bank, and state control over its operations, or nationalization of the banks.

(2) Nationalization of the syndicates, i.e., the largest, monopolistic capitalist associations (sugar, oil, coal, iron and steel, and other syndicates).

(3) Abolition of commercial secrecy.

(4) Compulsory syndication (i.e., compulsory amalgamation into associations) of industrialists, merchants and employers generally.

(5) Compulsory organization of the population into consumers' societies, or encouragement of such organization, and the exercise of control over it.

12

From *One of the Fundamental Questions of the Revolution*

September 27 (October 10), 1917

Lenin never put aside the idea of the dictatorship of the proletariat. He repeated the need for such a dictatorship in this selection from an article published only weeks before the Bolsheviks took power.

The key question of every revolution is undoubtedly the question of state power. Which class holds power decides everything. . . .

The question of power cannot be evaded or brushed aside, because it is the key question determining *everything* in a revolution's development, and in its foreign and domestic policies. . . .

Only if power is based, obviously and unconditionally, *on a majority* of the population can it be stable during a popular revolution, i.e., a revolution which rouses the people, the majority of the workers and peasants, to action. . . .

What is now necessary in Russia is not to invent "new reforms," not to make "plans" for "comprehensive" changes. Nothing of the kind. This is how the situation is depicted—deliberately depicted in a false light—by the capitalists . . . who shout against "introducing socialism" and against the "dictatorship of the proletariat." The situation in Russia in fact is such that the unprecedented burdens and hardships of the war, the unparalleled and very real danger of economic dislocation and famine have of themselves suggested the way out, have of themselves not only pointed out, but advanced reforms and other changes as absolutely necessary. These changes must be the grain monopoly, control over production and distribution, restriction of the issue of paper money, a fair exchange of grain for manufactured goods, etc. . . .

What would such a dictatorship mean in practice? . . . Two days after its creation ninety-nine per cent of the army would be enthusiastic supporters of this dictatorship. This dictatorship would give land to the peasants and full power to the local peasant committees. . . .

V. I. Lenin, *Collected Works*, vol. 25 (Moscow: Progress Publishers, 1964), 366–67, 371, 373.

Only the dictatorship of the proletariat and the poor peasants is capable of smashing the resistance of the capitalists, of displaying truly supreme courage and determination in the exercise of power, and of securing the enthusiastic, selfless and truly heroic support of the masses both in the army and among the peasants.

Power to the Soviets—*this is the only way to make further progress gradual, peaceful and smooth,* keeping perfect pace with the political awareness and resolve of the majority of the people and with their own experience. Power to the Soviets means the complete transfer of the country's administration and economic control into the hands of the workers and peasants, to whom *nobody* would dare offer resistance and who, through practice, through their own experience, *would soon learn* how to distribute the land, products and grain properly.

2

The Monopolization of Power
during the Civil War: 1917–1920

The Bolsheviks faced armed opposition from late 1917 until November 1920. Lenin applied the term *civil war* broadly (Document 15). He envisaged a titanic struggle of the proletariat with the possessing classes, not only in Russia, but all over the world. In practice, the Civil War was both a context and a rationale for the concentration of power in the hands of a few Bolshevik leaders and for the institutionalization of a repressive regime (Documents 22 and 25). Lenin's personal role in banning rival parties, arresting their leaders, and in demonstrative arrests and summary executions is apparent in several of the documents.

The Civil War was total war (see Documents 35–37). Lenin sought to destroy the old regime, weaken its supporters, and secure power, as well as to provision the Red Army. Under the slogan "expropriation of expropriators," he promoted the nationalization of industry and the peasants' seizure of land. Although he had promised workers control over their factories, he soon subordinated the industrial and commercial sectors to the state and party apparatus. His rural policy evolved similarly. He urged the seizure and socialization of land, but then in the spring of 1918, he established a grain monopoly, forcing peasants to sell their crops to the state at artificially low prices or simply to hand over their grain to armed detachments. Decrees in May–June 1918 led to a state monopoly over the food supply. This was the embryo of the future policy of war communism and of the command economy. Neither the economy nor the political system that developed was preordained, and readers should weigh Lenin's ideological inclinations and leadership abilities against other factors, including luck and happenstance.

Toward One-Party Power

13

From *To Workers, Soldiers, and Peasants!*

October 25 (November 7), 1917

In this appeal, which was sanctioned by the Second All-Russian Congress of Soviets, Lenin notes the overthrow of the provisional government and the arrest of its members, many of whom were leaders of leftist or centrist parties. He does not, however, mention the Bolshevik Party, which had begun to rule under the cloak of "soviet power": that is, under the power of the soviets of Petrograd and other cities as in the Bolsheviks' slogan: All power to the soviets.

The Second All-Russian Congress of Soviets of Workers' and Soldiers' Deputies has opened. The vast majority of the Soviets are represented at the Congress. A number of delegates from the Peasants' Soviets are also present. The mandate of the compromising Central Executive Committee has terminated.[1] Backed by the will of the vast majority of the workers, soldiers and peasants, backed by the victorious uprising of the workers and the garrison which has taken place in Petrograd, the Congress takes power into its own hands.

The Provisional Government has been overthrown. The majority of the members of the Provisional Government have already been arrested....

The Congress decrees: all power in the localities shall pass to the Soviets of Workers', Soldiers' and Peasants' Deputies, which must guarantee genuine revolutionary order.

---

[1]The Central Executive Committee of the Soviet was elected at the First All-Russian Congress of Soviets in June 1917. The majority was in the hands of Mensheviks and SRs. At the Second All-Russian Congress of Soviet in late October and early November, the new All-Russian Central Executive Committee was elected, including only Bolsheviks and left SRs.

V. I. Lenin, *Collected Works*, vol. 26 (Moscow: Progress Publishers, 1964), 247–48.

14

From *Resolution of the Central Committee of the RSDLP(B) on the Opposition within the Central Committee*

November 2 (15), 1917

Lenin's first government consisted only of Bolsheviks. Yet when he felt that troops under the former premier Kerensky and General Krasnov threatened Bolshevik rule,[2] he negotiated with the Mensheviks and Socialist-Revolutionaries to form a coalition. The accord reached specified that neither Lenin nor Trotsky would enter the new government. When the counterrevolutionary attacks failed, he renounced the agreement. Several leading Bolsheviks wished the party to abide by the accord, but Lenin rallied a majority to his side. Lenin outsmarted his opponents in this case as in others, and his colleagues never again raised the idea of a coalition. In the following resolution, he and his supporters expressed their hostility to the coalition as well as their contempt for those who supported it.

The Central Committee considers that the present meeting is of historic importance and that it is therefore necessary to record the two positions which have been revealed here.

1. The Central Committee considers that the opposition formed within the Central Committee has departed completely from all the fundamental positions of Bolshevism and of the proletarian class struggle in general by reiterating the utterly un-Marxist talk of the impossibility of a socialist revolution in Russia and of the necessity of yielding to the ultimatums and threats of resignation on the part of the obvious minority in the Soviet organization, thus thwarting the will and the decision of the Second All-Russian Congress of Soviets and sabotaging the dictatorship of the proletariat and the poor peasantry which has been inaugurated.

2. The Central Committee lays the whole responsibility for hindering

[2]Petr Nikolaevich Krasnov (1869–1947), a Russian general. In 1918, he was the leader of the Don Cossaks. In 1919, he emigrated to Germany.

V. I. Lenin, *Collected Works*, vol. 26 (Moscow: Progress Publishers, 1964), 277–78.

revolutionary work and for the vacillations, so criminal at the present moment, on this opposition, and invites them to transfer their discussion and their skepticism to the press and to withdraw from the practical work they do not believe in. For this opposition reflects nothing but intimidation by the bourgeoisie and the sentiments of the exhausted (not the revolutionary) section of the population.

3. The Central Committee affirms that the purely Bolshevik government cannot be renounced without betraying the slogan of Soviet power, since the majority at the Second All-Russian Congress of Soviets, without excluding anybody from the Congress, entrusted power, to this government.

15

Decree on the Arrest of the Leaders of the Civil War against the Revolution

November 28 (December 11), 1917

There were several steps in the establishment of the one-party dictatorship. One was the banishment of the Cadet Party and the arrest of its leaders. This was done under a special decree written by Lenin. This brief document is important for Lenin's condemnation of the Cadet Party as a "party of the enemies of the people," a phrase he soon applied to all opponents, and as a step curtailing independent political activity.

Members of leading bodies of the Cadet Party, as a party of enemies of the people, are liable to arrest and trial by revolutionary tribunal.

Local Soviets are ordered to exercise special surveillance over the Cadet Party in view of its connection with the Kornilov-Kaledin civil war against the revolution.

This decree enters into effect from the time of signing.

V. Ulyanov (Lenin),
Chairman of the Council of People's Commissars

V. I. Lenin, *Collected Works*, vol. 26 (Moscow: Progress Publishers, 1964), 351.

16

From *Draft Decree on the Dissolution of the Constituent Assembly*

January 6 (19), 1918

The dissolution of the Constituent Assembly was an important step in Lenin's consolidation of absolute rule. The convocation of a Constituent Assembly was a historic demand of Russian revolutionaries. The Bolsheviks promised to convene it and permitted the election of delegates to the Assembly in December 1917. At this time, the Bolsheviks were supported by a faction of the Socialist Revolutionary Party that had split from their party in late 1917 over support for the revolution and had established the Party of Left Socialist-Revolutionaries (Left SRs). The Left SRs did not join the Bolshevik government, but did support the Bolsheviks in elections to the Assembly and later held secondary positions in the government and other administrative bodies. The Bolsheviks and their Left SR allies won roughly a quarter of the votes in the election, mostly in the cities, but the center and right SRs won a majority, and with it, control of the Assembly. The Constituent Assembly convened on January 5 (18), 1918, but refused to confirm the decrees of the Soviet government. Bolshevik Red Guards prevented delegates from entering the meeting hall the following day when the Assembly reconvened at noon. The Soviet government dispersed demonstrations in favor of the Constituent Assembly, and moderate SRs failed to rally enough support to challenge the Bolsheviks.

The main initiator of the dissolution of the Constituent Assembly was Lenin, who prepared the following decree that was adopted by the All-Russian Central Executive Committee on the night of January 6 (19), 1918.

At its very inception, the Russian revolution produced the Soviets of Workers', Soldiers' and Peasants' Deputies as the only mass organization of all the working and exploited classes capable of leading the struggle of these classes for their complete political and economic emancipation. . . .

V. I. Lenin, *Collected Works*, vol. 26 (Moscow: Progress Publishers, 1964), 434–36.

The Constituent Assembly, elected on the basis of electoral lists drawn up prior to the October Revolution, was an expression of the old relation of political forces which existed when power was held by the compromisers and the Cadets. When the people at that time voted for the candidates of the Socialist-Revolutionary Party, they were not in a position to choose between the Right Socialist-Revolutionaries, the supporters of the bourgeoisie, and the Left Socialist-Revolutionaries, the supporters of socialism. The Constituent Assembly, therefore, which was to have crowned the bourgeois parliamentary republic, was bound to become an obstacle in the path of the October Revolution and Soviet power.

The October Revolution, by giving power to the Soviets, and through the Soviets to the working and exploited classes, aroused the desperate resistance of the exploiters, and in the crushing of this resistance it fully revealed itself as the beginning of the socialist revolution. The working classes learned by experience that the old bourgeois parliamentary system had outlived its purpose and was absolutely incompatible with the aim of achieving socialism, and that not national institutions, but only class institutions (such as the Soviets) were capable of overcoming the resistance of the propertied classes and of laying the foundations of socialist society. To relinquish the sovereign power of the Soviets, to relinquish the Soviet Republic won by the people, for the sake of the bourgeois parliamentary system and the Constituent Assembly, would now be a step backwards and would cause the collapse of the October workers' and peasants' revolution.

Owing to the above-mentioned circumstances, the Party of Right Socialist-Revolutionaries, the party of Kerensky, Avksentyev,[3] and Chernov,[4] obtained the majority in the Constituent Assembly which met on January 5. Naturally, this party refused to discuss the absolutely clear, precise and unambiguous proposal of the supreme organ of Soviet power, the Central Executive Committee of the Soviets, to recognize the program of Soviet power, to recognize the Declaration of Rights of the Working and Exploited People,[5] to recognize

[3]Nikolai Dmitrievich Avksentyev (1878–1943), a leader of the SRs who emigrated after the Bolsheviks took power.
[4]Viktor Mikhailovich Chernov (1873–1952), a founder of the Socialist-Revolutionary Party and its main theorist. After 1917, he emigrated.
[5]"The Declaration of Rights of the Working and Exploited People" was adopted by the Third All-Russian Congress of Soviets on January 12 (25), 1918. It was included in the Constitution of Soviet Russia in 1918.

the October Revolution and Soviet power. By this action the Constituent Assembly severed all ties with the Soviet Republic of Russia. . . .

Accordingly, the Central Executive Committee resolves that the Constituent Assembly is hereby dissolved.

17

From *Speech to Propagandists on Their Way to the Provinces*

February 5, 1918

Institutionalizing Bolshevik authority in the countryside and maintaining the food supply were undoubtedly the Bolsheviks' two greatest challenges. Each presented its difficulties, but in the absence of anything to offer the peasants after the peasants had taken the land, the problem of getting the peasants' grain and produce to feed the urban populations and the army was the most intractable. Lenin hoped, as he says in this speech to activists on their way to the countryside, to win over the poorest strata of the villages with the promise that they would gain at the expense of their more prosperous neighbors by allying with his government. Since the divisions in the villages were not as sharp as he had supposed, however, the strategy largely failed, leading the government to seize grain and other produce forcefully in what amounted to a war against the peasants.

In this powerful speech, Lenin expresses his confidence in victory in the face of famine and chaos. He addresses those on whom everything would depend in the provinces, the local party workers, encouraging them, appealing to their idealism, and attempting to focus their anger and complaints on a vague conglomeration of class enemies, from the bourgeoisie and civil servants to "'bourgeois' peasants" and vagabonds. He particularly emphasizes the need to attack kulaks, *a word derived from the Russian word for* fist *and ordinarily applied to peasants who had gained wealth as money lenders. In this instance, Lenin applies the term to include all prosperous peasants, as well as those who sided with them or simply opposed his plans. Lenin's evocation of class conflict*

V. I. Lenin, *Collected Works*, vol. 26 (Moscow: Progress Publishers, 1964), 514–15.

raises the issue of the roles of the Bolshevik leaders, activists, and the villagers themselves in the brutal struggles that ensued.

Comrades, you have before you some very difficult but, as I have said, satisfying work which boils down to getting the rural economy running and building up Soviet power. But you have assistants, for we know that every worker and peasant earning his own livelihood feels, deep down in his heart, that there is no salvation from famine and ruin but in Soviet power. We can save Russia. There is every indication that Russia has the grain, and it would have been available if we had taken stock of it in good time and distributed it fairly. Cast your mind's eye over the boundless expanse of Russia and her disrupted railways and you will realize that we need to tighten up the control and distribution of grain, if this famine is not to be the end of us all. This can be done only on one condition, which is that each worker, each peasant and each citizen must understand that he has no one to look to but himself. Comrades, no one is going to help you. All the bourgeoisie, the civil servants, the saboteurs are against you, for they know that if the people manage to share out among themselves this national wealth which had been in the hands of the capitalists and the kulaks, they will rid Russia of the chaff and the drones. . . .

That is the job you have, that is where you must work to unite, organize and establish Soviet power. Out there in the countryside you will come across "bourgeois" peasants, the kulaks, who will try to upset Soviet power. It will be easy to fight them because the mass will be on your side. They will see that it is not punitive expeditions but propagandists that are sent from the center to bring light to the countryside, to unite those in every village who earn their own livelihood and have never lived at the expense of others.

Take the question of land: it has been declared public property and all types of private property are being abolished. This marks a great step towards the elimination of exploitation.

There will be a struggle between the rich and the working peasants, and it is not bookish help that the poor need but experience and actual participation in the struggle. We did not take away the land from the landowners to let the rich peasants and the kulaks get it. It is for the poor. This will win you the sympathies of the poor peasants.

You must see to it that farm implements and machines do not remain in the hands of the kulaks and rich peasants. They must belong to Soviet power and be temporarily allotted to the working peasants for their use, through the volost [county] committees. . . .

Every peasant will help you in this difficult task. You must explain to the people in the villages that the kulaks and sharks must be pulled up short. There is need for an even distribution of products so that the working people can enjoy the fruits of the people's labor. . . .

The external war is over or nearly so. There is no doubt on that score. It is an internal war that is now before us.

18

Interview Granted to an Izvestia *Correspondent in Connection with the Left Socialist-Revolutionary Revolt*

July 8, 1918

The Left SRs condemned the Bolsheviks for signing a separate peace treaty with Germany at Brest-Litovsk on March 3, 1918, in which the Soviet Republic lost considerable territory. The Left SRs' clash with the government led to the assassination in Moscow of the German ambassador to Soviet Russia, Count Whilhelm von Mirbach, on July 6, 1918, and the mysterious, brief arrest of F. E. Dzerzhinsky, chairman of the All-Russian Extraordinary Commission for Struggle against Counterrevolution, Sabotage, and Speculation (the security police, known after its Russian abbreviation as the VChK). The meaning of these events, which the Bolsheviks used as a pretext to destroy the Left SRs, the last large noncommunist party, remains unclear. It is possible that the Bolsheviks themselves engineered the assassination in order to suppress the Left SRs or that the event reflected a struggle within the Bolshevik Party.[6] The result in any case was that Russia was governed as a one-party state after mid-1918. Although the Mensheviks and Left SRs were not formally banned until the early 1920s, they lost their influence much earlier.

[6]Yuru Fel'shtinsky, *Vozhdi v Zakone* (Moscow: Terra, 1999), 126–75.

V. I. Lenin, *Collected Works*, vol. 27 (Moscow: Progress Publisher, 1964), 534–35.

Lenin condemns the Left SR's "terrorist acts" in the Izvestia[7] *interview that follows. Since the Bolsheviks themselves employed violent means, it is worth asking whether Lenin uses this phrase primarily to vilify the Left SRs or to justify a counterterror by the Bolsheviks themselves.*

Revolution with remarkable consistency drives every proposition to its logical conclusion and ruthlessly exposes the utter futility and criminality of all wrong tactics.

The Left Socialist-Revolutionaries, carried away by high-sounded phrases, have for several months now been screaming: "Down with the Brest peace! To arms against the Germans!"

We replied that under present conditions, in the present period of history, the Russian people cannot fight and do not want to fight.

Closing their eyes to the facts, they continued with insane obstinacy to persist in their own line, not sensing that they were drawing further and further away from the masses of the people, and determined at all costs, even by brute force, to impose their will on these masses, the will of their Central Committee, which included criminal adventurers, hysterical intellectuals, and so on.

And the further they drew away from the people, the more they earned the sympathies of the bourgeoisie, which was hoping to accomplish its designs by their hand.

Their criminal terrorist act[8] and revolt have fully and completely opened the eyes of the broad masses to the abyss into which the criminal tactics of the Left Socialist-Revolutionary adventurers are dragging Soviet Russia, the Russia of the people.

On the day of the revolt, I myself and many other comrades had occasion to hear even the most backward sections of the people expressing their profound disgust of the Left Socialist-Revolutionaries.

One simple old woman said indignantly on hearing of the assassination of Mirbach: "The devils, so they've driven us into war after all!"

It at once became perfectly clear and obvious to everybody that the Socialist-Revolutionaries' terroristic act had brought Russia to the

---

[7]*Izvestia* (The News) was the newspaper of the All-Russian Central Executive Committee from 1917. After November 1917, it was supervised by the Bolshevik leadership.

[8]Lenin had in mind the murder of the German ambassador in Moscow, Count Mirbakh, by the Left SR Yakov Blumkin on July 6, 1918. The murder provided a pretext for the prohibition of the Party of Left Socialist-Revolutionaries.

brink of war. That, in fact, was what the masses thought of the action of the Left Socialist-Revolutionaries.

They are trying by underhand methods to embroil us in war with the Germans at a time when we cannot fight and do not want to fight. The masses will never forgive the Left Socialist-Revolutionaries for trampling so brutally on the will of the people and trying to force them into war.

And if anybody was well pleased with the action of the Left Socialist-Revolutionaries and rubbed his hands with glee, it was only the white-guards and the servitors of the imperialist bourgeoisie; whereas the worker and peasant masses have been rallying ever closer and more solidly around the Communist-Bolshevik Party, the authentic spokesman of the will of the masses.

The Bolshevik Terror and the Stigmatization of Public Enemies

19

Draft Resolution on Freedom of the Press
November 4 (17), 1917

One-party power required the forcible suppression of all political opposition, and the Bolsheviks employed terror against their opponents from their first days in power. Lenin and his government viewed the press as a weapon in the struggle for power and wrote the following document within ten days of seizing power.[9]

[9]On October 26 (November 8), the Revolutionary Military Committee closed down a number of newspapers. The next day the Council of People's Commissars adopted the decree on the press that confirmed the Bolshevik monopoly over the printed word. On November 4 (17), the All-Russian Central Executive Committee discussed the question because some members opposed the decree, but after a short discussion Lenin's resolution was adopted.

V. I. Lenin, *Collected Works*, vol. 26 (Moscow: Progress Publishers, 1964), 283.

For the bourgeoisie, freedom of the press meant freedom for the rich to publish and for the capitalists to control the newspapers, a practice, which in all countries, including even the freest, produced a corrupt press.

For the workers' and peasants' government, freedom of the press means liberation of the press from capitalist oppression, and public ownership of paper mills and printing presses; equal right for public groups of a certain size (say, numbering 10,000) to a fair share of newsprint stocks and a corresponding quantity of printers' labor.

As a first step toward this goal, which is bound up with the working people's liberation from capitalist oppression, the Provisional Workers' and Peasants' Government has appointed a Commission of Inquiry to look into the ties between capital and periodicals, the sources of their funds and every other aspect of the newspaper business in general. Concealment of books, accounts or any other documents from the Commission of Inquiry, or the giving of any evidence known to be false shall be punishable by a revolutionary court.

All newspaper owners, shareholders, and all members of their staffs shall be under the obligation to immediately submit written reports and information on the said questions to the *Commission of Inquiry*, probing the ties between capital and the press, and its dependence on capital, at Smolny Institute, Petrograd.

The following are appointed to serve on the Commission of Inquiry:[10]

The Commission shall have the power to co-opt members, call experts, subpoena witnesses, order the presentation of all accounts, etc.

---

[10]There follows space for a list of names. [Note of Editors of Lenin's *Collected Works*.]

20

Letter to G. I. Blagonravov and V. D. Bonch-Bruevich

December 8 (21), 1917

Lenin denounced critics and opponents as class enemies and "enemies of the people." Again and again during his first months in power he urged draconian measures and railed against those inclined to leniency. On December 7 (20), 1917, he asked Polish communist F. E. Dzerzhinsky to work on a decree on the struggle with counterrevolutionary saboteurs.[11] The same day the All-Russian Extraordinary Commission for Struggle against Counterrevolution, Sabotage, and Speculation (known after its Russian abbreviation as VChK) was created. Dzerzhinsky became its chairman and soon developed a reputation for pitilessness as in his reputed authorization in 1921 of the summary execution of N. S. Gumilev, one of Russia's greatest twentieth-century poets.[12] The VChK received exclusive rights to administer "justice" and punish opponents by any means, including shooting them without a trial, taking hostages, and incarcerating them in forced-labor camps. In contrast to the later Nazi concentration camps, which were designed to exterminate Jews and other "undesirables," the first Soviet camps were set up to exclude enemies from society and exploit their labor, though in the end many died.

The VChK began making arrests in Petrograd the day after its creation. Lenin's role in these measures is evident from this letter recommending police measures.

---

[11]Yu. G. Fel'shtinsky, ed., *VChK-GPU, Dokumenty I Materialy* (Moscow: Izdatel'stvo gumanitarnoi literatury, 1995).

[12]Solomon Volkov, *St. Petersburg: A Cultural History*, trans. Antonina W. Bouis (New York: The Free Press, 1995), 234–35.

V. I. Lenin, *Collected Works*, vol. 44 (Moscow: Progress Publishers, 1970), 49.

Comrades Blagonravov and Bonch-Bruevich,[13]

The arrests which have to be carried out on the order of Comrade Peters[14] are of *exceptionally* great importance and must be executed with great energy. *Special* measures must be taken to prevent destruction of papers, flight, concealment of documents, etc.

V. Ulyanov (Lenin)
Chairman, Council of People's Commissars

21

Telegram to V. L. Paniushkin
June 15, 1918

Lenin was the first among the Bolshevik leadership to demand mass arrests and executions of opponents. He considered arrests a good indicator of his envoys' work in the provinces, as seen in this telegram to V. L. Paniushkin, a Bolshevik and the extraordinary commissar in Tula for the struggle against the counterrevolution, in June 1918.

[I am] surprised [by] the absence of news. Inform [me] quickly how much grain is poured out [into containers?], how many [goods] wagons are sent, how many speculators and kulaks are arrested.

Lenin
Chairman of the Council of People's Commissars

---

[13]Grigorii Ivanovich Blagonravov (1895–1937) was a Bolshevik member of the Revolutionary Military Council of the Eastern Front in 1918. Vladimir Dmitrievich Bonch-Bruevich (1873–1955) was a Bolshevik and in 1917–1920 was the manager for affairs of the Council of People's Commissars of the Russian Federation.
[14]Yakov Khristoforovich Peters (1886–1837) was one of the leaders of VChK from the first months of its existence.

V. I. Lenin, *Polnoe Sobranie Sochinenii*, 4th ed., vol. 50 (Moscow: Politizdat, 1965), 89.

Letter to G. E. Zinoviev

June 26, 1918

In late June 1918, Lenin wrote indignantly to G. E. Zinoviev, the head of the Petrograd party organization, and other Petrograd leaders about the murder of V. Volodarsky, the city's commissar for press affairs, urging repression of all who opposed Bolshevik rule. Note his eagerness to intimidate possible opponents.

Also to Lashevich[15] and other members of the CC.

Com[rade] Zinoviev! Only today we have heard in the CC that in Piter [Petrograd] workers wanted to answer the murder of Volodarsky with mass terror and that you (not personally but Piter Chekists and Piter Committee's members) restrained [them].

[I am] protesting decisively!

We are compromising ourselves: we threaten mass terror even in resolutions of the Soviet of Deputies, but when it comes to the action, [we] hamper the revolutionary initiative of the masses, entirely correct.

It is im-pos-sible!

The terrorists will consider us spineless creatures; the time is extreme-military. It is necessary to invoke the energy and mass scale of the terror against counterrevolutionaries, and especially in Piter, the example of which will be decisive.

Cheers! *Lenin*

[15]Mikhail Mikhailovich Lashevich (1884–1928) was a member of the CC and a military official who worked at that time in Petrograd.

V. I. Lenin, *Polnoe Sobranie Sochinenii*, 4th ed., vol. 50 (Moscow: Progress Publishers, 1970), 106.

From *Report of the Council of People's Commissars on the Fifth All-Russian Congress of Soviets*

July 5, 1918

Lenin adamantly eschewed leniency toward his enemies even in the face of widespread famine and threats from foreign powers. One dangerous moment for the Bolsheviks came in the summer of 1918, when Czech soldiers, prisoners of war who had been transferred to the far eastern region of the Russian Empire, rebelled against the Bolshevik regime. Their insurrection was supported by anti-Bolshevik forces on the Volga River, in the Ural Mountains, and in Siberia. The Allies encouraged the Czechs and mutinous Russians by sending some military supplies and small detachments of troops. The Czechs had some brief success, but with only limited support from Britain and France, the Red Army soon overwhelmed them.

A terrible disaster—famine—has befallen us, and the more difficult our situation, the more acute the food crisis, the more the capitalists intensify their struggle against Soviet power. You know that the Czechoslovak mutiny is a mutiny of men who have been bought by the British and French imperialists. We are constantly hearing of revolts against the Soviets in one place or another. The kulak risings[16] are spreading from region to region. In the Don region, there is Krasnov, whom the Russian workers magnanimously allowed to go free in Petrograd when he came and surrendered his sword, for the prejudices of the intellectual are still strong and the intellectuals protested against capital punishment—Krasnov was allowed to go free because of the intellectual's prejudice against capital punishment. But I would like to see the people's court today, the workers' or peasants' court, which would not sentence Krasnov, who is shooting workers and peas-

---

[16]*Kulak* was a scornful term for a wealthy peasant. The Bolshevik leadership proclaimed the kulaks to be the main enemy in the countryside. Lenin and his subordinates designated the peasant revolt against them as a "kulak uprising."

V. I. Lenin, *Collected Works*, vol. 27 (Moscow: Progress Publishers, 1964), 518–19.

ants, to be shot. We are told that when people are sentenced to be shot by Dzerzhinsky's commission[17] it is all right, but if a court were to declare publicly and openly that a man was a counterrevolutionary and deserved to be shot, that would be wrong. People who have sunk to such depths of hypocrisy are political corpses. (*Applause.*) No, a revolutionary who does not want to be a hypocrite cannot renounce capital punishment. There has never been a revolution or a period of civil war without shootings.

24

Telegram to the Penza Gubernia Executive Committee of the Soviets

August 19, 1918

The famine sparked increased opposition in the countryside, and Lenin urged the ruthless suppression of peasants who opposed the confiscation of grain by Bolshevik military detachments, a subject covered more fully in the section on War Communism. The following telegram to functionaries in the city of Penza reveals Lenin's expectation that his subordinates would employ violent means.

August 19, 1918

Gubernia Executive Committee
Penza
Copy to the Gubernia Committee of the Communists

I am extremely indignant that there has been absolutely nothing definite from you as to what serious measures have at last been carried out by you for ruthless suppression of the kulaks of five volosts [counties] and confiscation of their grain. Your inactivity is criminal. All

[17]The Cheka, the secret police.

V. I. Lenin, *Collected Works*, vol. 44 (Moscow: Progress Publishers, 1970), 135.

efforts should be concentrated on a single volost [county] which should be swept clean of all grain surpluses. Telegraph fulfilment.

Lenin
Chairman, Council of People's Commissars

25

From *Letter to Maxim Gorky*
September 15, 1919

Lenin used intellectuals as specialists in industry and the military and as propagandists, but always suspected them of disloyalty as a group. He expressed his scorn and contempt with the term "bourgeois intelligentsia." The writer Maxim Gorky is a good example. Gorky was probably the most famous Russian writer in 1917. He had been an early Bolshevik advocate, but opposed the revolution because he feared it would lead to barbarism in a country with such a small educated elite. When he returned to the Bolshevik fold, however, he was allotted some power in cultural affairs. The relationship between Lenin and Gorky was mutually advantageous. Lenin drew on Gorky's prestige, and the writer succeeded in saving some leading figures in literature and the arts from starvation. Sometimes, Gorky asked Lenin to rescue an arrested or victimized artist or writer, and, in rare cases, Lenin complied. Usually, Lenin refused Gorky's demands, however, or simply ignored them. In the following letter, Lenin lectures Gorky on the need for "red terror" and the unreliability of bourgeois intellectuals.

It is also clear that in general the measure of arrest applied to Cadet (and near-Cadet) people has been necessary and correct.

Reading your frank opinion on this matter, I recall a remark of yours, which sank into my mind during our talks (in London, on Capri, and afterwards):

"We artists are irresponsible people."

Exactly! You utter incredibly angry words about what? About a few dozen (or perhaps even a few hundred) Cadet and near-Cadet gentry spending a few days in jail *in order to prevent plots like that of the surrender of Krasnaya Gorka,*[18] plots which threaten the lives of *tens* of thousands of workers and peasants.

A calamity, indeed! What injustice! A few days, or even weeks, in jail for intellectuals in order to prevent the massacre of tens of thousands of workers and peasants!

"Artists are irresponsible people."

It is wrong to confuse the "intellectual forces" of the people with the "forces" of bourgeois intellectuals. As a sample of the latter I take Korolenko:[19] I recently read the pamphlet *War, the Fatherland and Mankind,* which he wrote in August 1917. Mind you, Korolenko is the best of the "near-Cadets," almost a Menshevik. But what a disgusting, base, vile defense of imperialist war, concealed behind honeyed phrases! A wretched philistine in thrall to bourgeois prejudices! For such gentlemen 10,000,000 killed in an imperialist war is a deed worthy of support (by *deeds,* accompanied by honeyed phrases "against" war), but the death of hundreds of thousands in a *just* civil war against the landowners and capitalists evokes ahs and ohs, sighs, and hysterics.

No. There is no harm in such "talents" being made to spend some weeks or so in prison, if this *has* to be done to *prevent* plots (like Krasnaya Gorka) and the death of tens of thousands. But we exposed these plots of the Cadets and "near-Cadets." And we *know* that the near-Cadet professors quite often *help* the plotters. That's a fact.

The intellectual forces of the workers and peasants are growing and gaining strength in the struggle to overthrow the bourgeoisie and its henchmen, the intellectual lackeys of capital, who imagine they are the brains of the nation. Actually, they are not the brains, but sh[it].[20]

Problems of War and World Revolution

Two external issues shaped the Bolsheviks' rise to power and their development of the Soviet state and its policies. The first was World War I, which continued in Russia for almost five months after October

---

[18]Krasnaya Gorka was a fort in the Finnish gulf where in June 1919 the anti-Bolshevik mutiny took place. The Red Army suppressed it.

[19]V. G. Korolenko (1853–1921) was a novelist, a journalist, and an editor who criticized the Bolshevik terror.

[20]Lenin used only the first letter of the Russian expletive *govno.*

1917 and in other countries for a whole year. The war ended only in November 1918. The second issue was revolution abroad, which Bolshevik leaders hoped would begin once they broke the chain of world imperialism.

Only Lenin and a few others among the leaders and potential leaders of Russia understood that continuing the war with Germany was impossible. The soldiers did not want to fight, and the Russian army was disintegrating. Although some left-minded Bolsheviks (Trotsky, Bukharin, and others) tried to turn the imperialist war into a "revolutionary" war that working people in the West would support, Lenin was more circumspect, and he got his way. While the party argued, negotiations ceased and German troops continued to advance. At Lenin's behest, negotiations resumed. On March 3, 1918, the Treaty of Brest-Litovsk was signed between Germany and the Soviet Republic and was soon approved by the party and soviet congresses. Russia gave up rich industrial and agricultural lands including Finland, Russian Poland, the Baltic States, Ukraine, and much of Belorussia. The treaty was harsh, but it was the best strategy to ensure the survival of the Bolshevik regime.

26

The Socialist Fatherland Is in Danger!
February 21, 1918

In the following decree, Lenin articulates his position on the war with Germany, his desire for a treaty, and his belief in the coming world revolution.

In order to save this exhausted and ravaged country from new ordeals of war we decided to make a very great sacrifice and informed the Germans of our readiness to sign their terms of peace. Our truce envoys left Rezhitsa for Dvinsk in the evening on February 20 (7), *and still there is no reply*. The German Government is evidently in no hurry to reply. It obviously does not want peace. Fulfilling the task

V. I. Lenin, *Collected Works*, vol. 27 (Moscow: Progress Publishers, 1964), 30, 33.

with which it has been charged by the capitalists of all countries, German militarism *wants to strangle the Russian and Ukrainian workers and peasants, to return the land to the landowners, the mills and factories to the bankers, and power to the monarchy.* The German generals want to establish their "order" in Petrograd and Kiev. *The Socialist Republic of Soviets is in gravest danger.* Until the proletariat of Germany rises and triumphs, it is the sacred duty of the workers and peasants of Russia devotedly to defend the Republic of Soviets against the hordes of bourgeois-imperialist Germany. The Council of People's Commissars resolves: (1) *The country's entire manpower and resources are placed entirely at the service of revolutionary defense.* (2) *All Soviets and revolutionary organizations are ordered to defend every position to the last drop of blood.* (3) Railway organizations and the Soviets associated with them must do their utmost to prevent the enemy from availing himself of the transport system; in the event of a retreat, they are to destroy the tracks and blow up or burn down the railway buildings; all rolling stock—carriages and locomotives—must be immediately dispatched eastward, into the interior of the country. (4) All grain and food stocks generally, as well as all valuable property in danger of falling into the enemy's hands, must be unconditionally destroyed; the duty of seeing that this is done is laid upon the local Soviets and their chairmen are made personally responsible. (5) The workers and peasants of Petrograd, Kiev, and of all towns, townships, villages and hamlets along the line of the new front are to mobilize battalions to dig trenches, under the direction of military experts. (6) *These battalions are to include all able-bodied members of the bourgeois class, men and women, under the supervision of Red Guards; those who resist are to be shot.* (7) All publications which oppose the cause of revolutionary defense and side with German bourgeoisie, or which endeavor to take advantage of the invasion of the imperialist hordes in order to overthrow Soviet rule, are to be suppressed; able-bodied editors and members of the staffs of such publications are to be mobilized for the digging of trenches or for other defense work. (8) *Enemy agents, profiteers, marauders, hooligans, counter-revolutionary agitators and German spies are to be shot on the spot.*

The Socialist fatherland is in danger! Long live the socialist fatherland! Long live the international socialist revolution!

Council of People's Commissars

27

V. I. LENIN AND OTHERS

From *Resolution on War and Peace*

March 8, 1918

Lenin had to argue and threaten his colleagues to convince them to support the unfavorable peace with Germany, but he was successful. The Extraordinary Seventh Party Congress (March 6–8, 1918) passed the resolution he wrote with G. Ye. Sokol'nikov and G. Ye. Zinoviev in which he reiterated his belief in the importance of terror and the centralization of power.

The Congress recognizes the necessity to confirm the extremely harsh, humiliating treaty with Germany that has been concluded by Soviet power in view of our lack of an army, in view of the most unhealthy state of the demoralized army at the front, in view of the need to take advantage of any, even the slightest, possibility of obtaining a respite before imperialism launches its offensive against the Soviet Socialist Republic.

In the present period of the era that has begun, the era of the socialist revolution, numerous military attacks on Soviet Russia by the imperialist powers (both from the West and from the East) are historically inevitable. The historical inevitability of such attacks at a time when both internal, class relations and international relations are extremely tense, can at any moment, even immediately, within the next few days, lead to fresh imperialist aggressive wars against the socialist movement in general and against the Russian Socialist Soviet Republic in particular.

The Congress therefore declares that it recognizes the primary and fundamental task of our Party, of the entire vanguard of the class-conscious proletariat and of Soviet power, to be the adoption of the most energetic, ruthlessly determined and Draconian measures to improve the self-discipline and discipline of the workers and peasants of Russia, to explain the inevitability of Russia's historic advance towards

V. I. Lenin, *Collected Works*, vol. 27 (Moscow: Progress Publishers, 1964), 118–19.

a socialist, patriotic war of liberation, to create everywhere soundly co-ordinated mass organizations held together by a single iron will, organizations that are capable of concerted, valorous action in their day-to-day efforts and especially at critical moments in the life of the people, and, lastly, to train systematically and comprehensively in military matters and military operations the entire adult population of both sexes.

The Congress considers the only reliable guarantee of consolidation of the socialist revolution that has been victorious in Russia to be its conversion into a world working-class revolution.

28

From *Letter to the Workers and Peasants apropos of the Victory over Kolchak*

August 24, 1919

The Bolsheviks provoked the ire of the great capitalist nations for many reasons. They nationalized foreign-owned industries, renounced Russia's foreign debt, and refused to honor the conventions of international trade and finance. Western leaders bridled at the Bolsheviks' use of terror and their efforts to foment revolution abroad. Yet the immediate impetus for foreign intervention in Russia was the separate peace with Germany. Russia's former allies, the British, French, and Americans, feared that Germany would shift forces to the western front and use Russian territory and resources in the war effort. For these reasons, they supported the anti-Bolshevik revolts that followed the October Revolution.

The struggle that ensued was bloody. The White generals A. V. Kolchak,[21] A. I. Denikin,[22] N. N. Yudenich,[23] and others tried to overthrow

---

[21] Aleksandr Vasilievich Kolchak (1874–1920), a Russian admiral and a leader of the Russian anti-Bolshevik resistance; in 1919–1920, he was Supreme ruler of the Russian state.

[22] Anton Ivanovich Denikin (1872–1947), a Russian general. In 1919–1920, he was commander in chief of the anti-Bolshevik Military Powers of the South of Russia.

[23] Nikolai Nikolaevich Yudenich (1862–1933), a Russian general. In 1919, he was commander-in-chief of the anti-Bolshevik North-Western Russian Army.

V. I. Lenin, *Collected Works*, vol. 29 (Moscow: Progress Publishers, 1964), 552–57.

the Bolshevik regime: They nearly succeeded. The British, French, Germans, Americans, and Japanese all aided the Whites at one time or another. Lenin anticipated a civil war in which the bourgeoisie and other hostile social groups would be destroyed. This expectation shaped his treatment of enemies. He never separated the Civil War from his dream of revolutionary transformation or from his hatred for his enemies. He expressed his conviction that victory depended on state control of the economy and repression of the opposition in the following document.

Comrades, Red troops have liberated the entire Urals area from Kolchak and have begun the liberation of Siberia. The workers and peasants of the Urals and Siberia are enthusiastically welcoming Soviet power, for it is sweeping away with an iron broom all the landowner and capitalist scum who ground down the people with exactions, humiliations, floggings, and the restoration of tsarist oppression.

Although we all rejoice at the liberation of the Urals and the entry of the Red troops into Siberia, we must not allow ourselves to be lulled into a sense of security. The enemy is still far from being destroyed. He has not even been definitely broken.

Every effort must be made to drive Kolchak and the Japanese and other foreign bandits out of Siberia, and even greater effort is needed to destroy the enemy, to prevent him from starting his banditry again and again.

How is that to be achieved?

The harrowing experience of the Urals and Siberia, as well as the experience of all countries which have been through the torments of the four years of imperialist war, must not be without its lessons for us. . . .

First lesson. In order to defend the power of the workers and peasants from the bandits, that is, from the landowners and capitalists, we need a powerful Red Army. We have proved—not by words but by actual deeds—that we are capable of creating it, that we have learned to direct it and to defeat the capitalists notwithstanding the lavish assistance in arms and equipment they are receiving from the richest countries in the world. That much the Bolsheviks have proved by actual deeds. . . .

Consequently, everyone who seriously wishes to rid himself of the rule of Kolchak must devote all his energies, means and ability without reservation to the task of building up and strengthening the Red Army. Obey all the laws on the Red Army and all orders conscientiously and scrupulously, support discipline in it in every way, and help the Red Army, each to the best of his ability—such is the prime, fundamental, and principal duty of every class-conscious worker and peasant who does not want the rule of Kolchak. . . .

Second lesson. The Red Army cannot be strong without large state stocks of grain, for without them it is impossible to move an army freely or to train it properly. Without them we cannot maintain the workers who are producing for the army.

Every class-conscious worker and peasant must know and remember that the chief reason now that our Red Army successes are not swift and stable enough is precisely the shortage of state stocks of grain. He who does not give his surpluses of grain to the state is helping Kolchak, he is a traitor and betrayer of the workers and peasants and is responsible for the unnecessary death and suffering of tens of thousands of workers and peasants in the Red Army.

Rogues and profiteers and very ignorant peasants argue in this way—better sell my grain at the open market price, I will get far more for it than the fixed paid by the state.

But the whole point is that free sale promotes profiteering; a few get rich, only the wealthy are sated, while the working masses go hungry. . . .

Third lesson. If Kolchak and Denikin are to be completely destroyed the strictest revolutionary order must be maintained, the laws and instructions of the Soviet government must be faithfully observed, and care must be taken that they are obeyed by all.

Kolchak's victories in Siberia and the Urals have been a clear example to all of us that the least disorder, the slightest infringement of Soviet laws, the slightest laxity or negligence at once serve to strengthen the landowners and capitalists and make for their victory. For the landowners and capitalists have not been destroyed and do not consider themselves vanquished; every intelligent worker and peasant sees, knows, and realizes that they have only been beaten and have gone into hiding, are lying low, very often disguising themselves by a "Soviet" "protective" coloring. Many landowners have wormed their way into state farms, and capitalists into various "chief administrations" and "central boards," acting the part of Soviet officials; they are watching every step of the Soviet government, waiting for it to make a mistake or show weakness, so as to overthrow it, to help the Czechoslovaks today and Denikin tomorrow. . . .

And in order to be able to catch them we must be skillful, careful, and class-conscious, we must watch out most attentively for the least disorder, for the slightest deviation from the conscientious observance of the laws of the Soviet government. . . .

Fourth lesson. It is criminal to forget not only that the Kolchak movement began with trifles but also that the Mensheviks ("Social-Democrats") and S.R.s ("Socialist-Revolutionaries") assisted its birth and directly supported it. It is time we learned to judge political parties not by their words, but by their deeds.

The Mensheviks and Socialist-Revolutionaries call themselves socialists, but they are actually *abettors of the counter-revolutionaries,* abettors of the landowners and capitalists. This was proved in practice not only by isolated facts, but by two big periods of the Russian revolution: (1) the Kerensky period, and (2) the Kolchak period. Both times the Mensheviks and Socialist-Revolutionaries, while professing to be "socialists" and "democrats," actually played the role of *abettors of the whiteguards.* Are we then going to be so foolish as to believe them now they are suggesting we let them "try again," and call our permission a "united socialist (or democratic) front"? Since the Kolchak experience, can there still be peasants other than few isolated individuals, who do not realize that a "united front" with the Mensheviks and Socialist Revolutionaries means union with the abettors of Kolchak? . . .

29

From *Letter to American Workers*
August 20, 1918

Although the Bolsheviks' first appeals for the overthrow of capitalism elsewhere were not successful, Lenin and his subordinates' continued to anticipate revolution abroad until the end of the Civil War in 1920.

This view had practical consequences. In the first months of Bolshevik rule, Lenin was convinced that its survival depended on the internal weaknesses of capitalist countries and conflicts among them. During the Civil War, he looked to the lower classes of the capitalist powers and national liberation movements in their colonies. He wrote several letters

V. I. Lenin, *Collected Works,* vol. 28 (Moscow: Progress Publishers, 1965), 74–75.

to workers of different countries, urging them to revolt. He believed they would learn from the Bolshevik example. Lenin appealed particularly to American workers in the following document.

We know that help from you will probably not come soon, comrade American workers, for the revolution is developing in different countries in different forms and at different tempos (and it cannot be otherwise). We know that although the European proletarian revolution has been maturing very rapidly lately, it may, after all, not flare up within the next few weeks. We are banking on the inevitability of the world revolution, but this does not mean that we are such fools as to bank on the revolution inevitably coming on a *definite* and early date. We have seen two great revolutions in our country, 1905 and 1917, and we know revolutions are not made to order, or by agreement. We know that circumstances brought *our* Russian detachment of the socialist proletariat to the fore not because of our merits, but because of the exceptional backwardness of Russia, and that *before* the world revolution breaks out a number of separate revolutions may be defeated.

In spite of this, we are firmly convinced that we are invincible, because the spirit of mankind will not be broken by the imperialist slaughter. Mankind will vanquish it. And the first country to *break* the convict chains of the imperialist war was *our* country. We sustained enormously heavy casualties in the struggle to break these chains, but we *broke* them. We are *free from* imperialist dependence, we have raised the banner of struggle for the complete overthrow of imperialism for the whole world to see.

We are now, as it were, in a besieged fortress, waiting for the other detachments of the world socialist revolution to come to our relief. These detachments *exist*, they are *more numerous* than ours, they are maturing, growing, gaining more strength the longer the brutalities of imperialism continue. The workers are breaking away from their social-traitors—the Gomperses, Hendersons, Renaudels, Scheidemanns and Renners.[24] Slowly but surely the workers are adopting communist, Bolshevik tactics and are marching towards the proletarian

---

[24]Samuel Gompers, Arthur Henderson, Pierre Renaudel, Philipp Scheidemann, and Karl Renner were at the time the leaders of social-democracy and trade unions in the United States, Great Britain, France, Germany, and Austria.

revolution, which alone is capable of saving dying culture and dying mankind.

In short, we are invincible, because the world proletarian revolution is invincible.

N. Lenin[25]

30

From *Speech at the Opening Session of the Congress*

March 2, 1919

Lenin imagined leading a European Soviet republic. The creation of this republic was an objective of the Communist International (Comintern), which was founded on his initiative in March 1919. This organization, although intended to promote revolution abroad, soon became largely an arm of Soviet policy. Opening the Comintern's First Congress, Lenin was optimistic about the prospects for European revolution.

Comrades, our gathering has great historic significance. It testifies to the collapse of all the illusions cherished by bourgeois democrats. Not only in Russia, but in the most developed capitalist countries of Europe, Germany for example, civil war is a fact.

The bourgeoisie are terror-stricken at the growing workers' revolutionary movement. This is understandable if we take into account that the development of events since the imperialist war inevitably favors the workers' revolutionary movement, and that the world revolution is beginning and growing in intensity everywhere.

The people are aware of the greatness and significance of the struggle now going on. All that is needed is to find the practical form to enable the proletariat to establish its rule. Such a form is the Soviet

[25]Lenin signed many books and articles with the initial *N*, which he never explained.

V. I. Lenin, *Collected Works*, vol. 28 (Moscow: Progress Publishers, 1965), 455.

system with the dictatorship of the proletariat. Dictatorship of the proletariat—until now those words were Latin to the masses. Thanks to the spread of the Soviets throughout the world this Latin has been translated into all modern languages; a practical form of dictatorship has been found by the working people.

31

From *"Left-Wing" Communism— an Infantile Disorder*
April–May 1920

Lenin's expectations for revolutions in the advanced industrial nations were not fulfilled. Uprisings in East Central Europe led to Soviet republics in Bavaria (Germany) and Hungary, but these were soon crushed. Recognizing that revolution in the West was a chimera, at least for a time, Lenin urged the new European communist parties to follow the Bolsheviks' lead. He expressed his altered view of the revolutionary process in the spring of 1920, on the eve of the Comintern's Second Congress, in his pamphlet "'Left-Wing' Communism—an Infantile Disorder."

In the first months after the proletariat in Russia had won political power (October 25 [November 7], 1917), it might have seemed that the enormous difference between backward Russia and the advanced countries of Western Europe would lead to the proletarian revolution in the latter countries bearing very little resemblance to ours. We now possess quite considerable international experience, which shows very definitely that certain fundamental features of our revolution have a significance that is not local, or peculiarly national, or Russian alone, but international. I am not speaking here of international significance in the broad sense of the term: not merely several but all the primary features of our revolution, and many of its secondary features, are of international significance in the meaning of its effect on

V. I. Lenin, *Collected Works*, vol. 31 (Moscow: Progress Publishers, 1965), 21.

all countries. I am speaking of it in the narrowest sense of the word, taking international significance to mean the international validity or the historical inevitability of a repetition, on an international scale, of what has taken place in our country. It must be admitted that certain fundamental features of our revolution do possess that significance.

It would, of course, be grossly erroneous to exaggerate this truth and to extend it beyond certain fundamental features of our revolution. It would also be erroneous to lose sight of the fact that, soon after the victory of the proletarian revolution in at least one of the advanced countries, a sharp change will probably come about: Russia will cease to be the model and will once again become a backward country (in the "Soviet" and the socialist sense).

32

From *Report on the International Situation and the Fundamental Tasks of the Communist International to the Second Congress of Comintern*

July 19, 1920

Disappointed in the industrialized West, Lenin turned to the colonized East, imagining uprisings against British imperialism and influence in India, Persia (Iran), and elsewhere. He expressed his general view of the revolutionary potential of colonial peoples in his address to the Second Congress of the Comintern (July–August, 1920). The Comintern emerged from this congress as a central organization designed to operate as a single worldwide Communist Party. The congress adopted a list of twenty-one conditions for inclusion in the Comintern. Among them were the requirements that parties centralize their governance according to the Bolshevik model of "democratic centralism"; break with reformists, social democrats, and, particularly, anyone who opposed the Soviet government; subordinate local trade unions to the party; periodically purge unreliable members; support the Soviet Republics; and accept as binding all decisions of the Comintern's Executive Committee. The result was to

V. I. Lenin, *Collected Works*, vol. 31 (Moscow: Progress Publishers, 1965), 233–34.

further the divide in the European left between those who had supported
their governments in World War I and those who had opposed them. In
his report, Lenin captures the fervor of this gathering of 217 delegates
from 41 countries who hoped for revolutions at home and to strike a
blow against international capitalism.

The groundwork has been laid for the Soviet movement all over the
East, all over Asia, among all the colonial peoples.

The proposition that the exploited must rise up against the
exploiters and establish their Soviets is not a very complex one. After
our experience, after two and a half years of the existence of the
Soviet Republic in Russia, and after the First Congress of the Third
International, this idea is becoming accessible to hundreds of millions
of people oppressed by the exploiters all over the world. We in Russia
are often obliged to compromise, to bide our time, since we are
weaker than the international imperialists, yet we know that we are
defending the interests of this mass of a thousand and a quarter million people. For the time being, we are hampered by barriers, prejudices and ignorance, which are receding into the past with every
passing hour; but we are more and more becoming representatives
and genuine defenders of this 70 per cent of the world's population,
this mass of working and exploited people. It is with pride that we can
say: at the First Congress we were in fact merely propagandists; we
were only spreading the fundamental ideas among the world's proletariat; we only issued the call for struggle; we were merely asking
where the people were who were capable of taking this path. Today
the advanced proletariat is everywhere with us. A proletarian army
exists everywhere, although sometimes it is poorly organized and
needs reorganizing. If our comrades in all lands help us now to organize a united army, no shortcomings will prevent us from accomplishing our task. That task is the world proletarian revolution, the creation
of a world Soviet republic. *(Prolonged applause.)*

33

From *Political Report to the Ninth All-Russian Conference of the RCP(B)*

September 20, 1920

As victory in the Civil War approached in the summer and fall of 1920, Lenin imagined the advance of the Red Army from Ukraine to Warsaw in Poland and then to Germany's capital, Berlin. For obvious reasons, he kept this hope secret. Such a military campaign would have violated Marx's precepts, as well as his own, and might have prompted a new foreign intervention. Yet when the Civil War seemed decided, the Poles, who had held back because they feared a White victory would lead to a strong and unfriendly Russian state, attacked. The Bolsheviks repulsed them, however, and for a moment the Red Army seemed ready to capture the Polish capital of Warsaw. Lenin expressed his excitement in the following report to the Ninth All-Russian Party Conference. The report was to be kept secret and did not appear in his collected works. His reference to the Treaty of Versailles (June 28, 1919), in which Germany and the Central Powers capitulated to the Allied Powers, may well indicate a hope that Soviet Russia could win the support of a revolutionary Germany that hoped to regain lands lost in the treaty to Poland.[26]

Soon after Lenin delivered this report, however, Soviet troops were defeated outside Warsaw. Lenin and the Bolshevik leadership recast their foreign policy and began to promote peaceful coexistence with capitalist countries. Peaceful coexistence was also the basis for a new domestic policy. Yet Lenin did not abandon plans for world revolution; he simply relegated them to the future.

And so, in sum, our conviction ripened that the Entente's military offensive against us was over, that the defensive war with imperialism had ended, and that we had won it. The stake was Poland. And Poland

---

[26]Richard Pipes, *Russia under the Bolshevik Regime* (New York: Vintage, 1995), 189–90.

Richard Pipes, ed., *The Unknown Lenin: From the Secret Archive* (New Haven, Conn., and London: Yale University Press, 1996), 97–98, 100–1.

thought that as a great power with imperialist traditions, she was capable of changing the nature of the war. This meant that the assessment was as follows: the period of defensive war was finished. (Please take fewer notes. This should not get into the press.) On the other hand, the offensive showed us that because the Entente was powerless to crush us militarily, powerless to utilize its troops, it could only push various small countries against us, countries that have no military worth and that maintain a landowner-bourgeois system only at the cost of such violence and terror as the Entente provides them with. . . .

Our advance proved that Poland could not beat us, but we were very close to [beating them]. It turned out that all this changed international politics. In approaching Warsaw, we came so close to the center of world imperialist politics that we started to make them [politics] ourselves. This sounds incomprehensible, but the history of the Council of Action in England[27] has proved with absolute precision that somewhere in the proximity of Warsaw lies not the center of the Polish bourgeois government and the republic of capital, but that somewhere in the proximity of Warsaw lies the center of the entire current system of international imperialism, and that we are now at a point when we are beginning to sway this system and making politics not in Poland, but in Germany and England. Thus in Germany and England we have created a completely new zone of the proletarian revolution against worldwide imperialism, because Poland, as a buffer between Russia and Germany, Poland, as the last state, will remain entirely in the hands of international imperialism against Russia. She is the linchpin of the whole Treaty of Versailles. The modern imperialist world rests on the Treaty of Versailles. . . .

We had tasked ourselves with occupying Warsaw; the task changed and it turned out that what was being decided was not the fate of Warsaw but the fate of the Treaty of Versailles.

---

[27]The Committee of Action was created by the leadership of the British Labor Party and trade unions in the summer of 1920 to stop Britain from aiding Poland during the Soviet-Polish war.

War Communism and the Invention of a Command Economy

34

From *The Immediate Tasks of the Soviet Government*

March–April 1918 (published in Pravda on April 28, 1918)

The Bolsheviks, including Lenin, lacked a clear economic policy when they took power. Lenin considered this issue for the first time in the spring of 1918, after divesting the great capitalists and landowners of their property, withdrawing the country from the world war, and winning the bitter struggle for power in the provinces and most of the empire. The issue was acute. Workers had seized control of factories with the Bolsheviks' encouragement, and peasants had divided up large estates in a process that involved score-settling and elemental social justice, as well as looting and murdering. These events led inexorably to economic decline and the threat of famine and social collapse. Lenin recognized the need for a new approach. In his essay "The Immediate Tasks of the Soviet Government," he ordered a halt to the offensive against capitalism and a temporary truce with part of the bourgeoisie. He used the term state capitalism *to imply a mixed economy in which the state controlled economic life, including the banks and large industry, while small owners and traders utilized market mechanisms. Yet he still wanted to maintain state control over the circulation of goods and services. This prefigured the future policy of War Communism. The following text illustrates one of the many instances in which ideology and practicality offer competing explanations for Lenin's position.*

The task of the day is to restore the productive forces destroyed by the war and by bourgeois rule; to heal the wounds inflicted by the war,

V. I. Lenin, *Collected Works*, vol. 27 (Moscow: Progress Publishers, 1964), 243–45, 248–49.

by the defeat in the war, by profiteering and the attempts of the bourgeoisie to restore the overthrown rule of the exploiters; to achieve economic revival; to provide reliable protection of elementary order. It may sound paradoxical, but in fact, considering the objective conditions indicated above, it is absolutely certain that at the present moment the Soviet system can secure Russia's transition to socialism only if these very elementary, extremely elementary problems of maintaining public life are practically solved in spite of the resistance of the bourgeoisie, the Mensheviks and the Right Socialist-Revolutionaries. In view of the specific features of the present situation, and in view of the existence of Soviet power with its land socialization law, workers' control law, etc., the practical solution of these extremely elementary problems and the overcoming of the organizational difficulties of the first stages of progress toward socialism are now two aspects of the same picture.

Keep regular and honest accounts of money, manage economically, do not be lazy, do not steal, observe the strictest labor discipline—it is these slogans, justly scorned by the revolutionary proletariat when the bourgeoisie used them to conceal its rule as the exploiting class, that are now, since the overthrow of the bourgeoisie, becoming the immediate and the principal slogans of the moment. On the one hand, the practical application of these slogans by *the mass* of working people is the *sole* condition for the salvation of a country which has been tortured almost to death by the imperialist war and by the imperialist robbers (headed by Kerensky); on the other hand, the practical application of these slogans by the *Soviet* state, by *its* methods, on the basis of *its* laws, is the necessary and *sufficient* condition for the final victory of socialism. This is precisely what those who contemptuously brush aside the idea of putting such "hackneyed" and "trivial" slogans in the forefront fail to understand. In a small-peasant country, which overthrew tsarism only a year ago, and which liberated itself from the Kerenskys less than six months ago, there has naturally remained not a little of spontaneous anarchy, intensified by the brutality and savagery that accompany every protracted and reactionary war, and there has arisen a good deal of despair and aimless bitterness. And if we add to this the provocative policy of the lackeys of the bourgeoisie (the Mensheviks, the Right Socialist-Revolutionaries, etc.) it will become perfectly clear what prolonged and persistent efforts must be exerted by the best and the most class-conscious workers and peasants in order to bring about a complete change in the mood of the people and to bring them on the proper path of steady and disciplined labor. Only such a transition brought about by the mass of the poor (the proletarians and semi-proletarians) can consummate the victory over the bourgeoisie and particularly over the peasant bourgeoisie, more stubborn and numerous. . . .

The decisive thing is the organization of the strictest and country-wide accounting and control of production and distribution of goods. And yet, we have *not yet* introduced accounting and control in those enterprises and in those branches and fields of economy which we have taken away from the bourgeoisie; and without this there can be no thought of achieving the second and equally essential material condition for introducing socialism, namely, raising the productivity of labor on a national scale. . . .

This is a peculiar epoch, or rather stage of development, and in order to defeat capital completely, we must be able to adapt the forms of our struggle to the peculiar conditions of this stage.

Without the guidance of experts in the various fields of knowledge, technology and experience, the transition to socialism will be impossible, because socialism calls for a conscious mass advance to greater productivity of labor compared with capitalism, and on the basis achieved by capitalism. Socialism must achieve this advance *in its own way*, by its own methods—or, to put it more concretely, by *Soviet* methods. And the specialists, because of the whole social environment which made them specialists, are, in the main, inevitably bourgeois. Had our proletariat, after capturing power, quickly solved the problem of accounting, control and organization on a national scale (which was impossible owing to the war and Russia's backwardness), then we, after breaking the sabotage, would also have completely subordinated these bourgeois experts to ourselves by means of universal accounting and control. Owing to the considerable "delay" in introducing accounting and control generally, we, although we have managed to conquer sabotage, have not yet created the conditions which would place the bourgeois specialists at our disposal. The mass of saboteurs are "going to work," but the best organizers and the top experts can be utilized by the state either in the old way, in the bourgeois way (i.e., for high salaries), or in the new way, in the proletarian way (i.e., creating the conditions of national accounting and control from below, which would inevitably and of itself subordinate the experts and enlist them for our work). . . .

Moreover, it is clear that this measure not only implies the cessation—in a certain field and to a certain degree—of the offensive against capital (for capital is not a sum of money, but a definite social relation); it is also a *step backward* on the part of our socialist Soviet state power, which from the very outset proclaimed and pursued the policy of reducing high salaries to the level of the wages of the average worker.

35

From *Organization of Food Detachments*
June 27, 1918

Peasants were reluctant to sell their surpluses because there were few manufactured goods to buy, and the rural economy continued to deteriorate. Lenin and many Bolsheviks, meanwhile, suspected the peasants of hostile intentions. The All-Russian Central Executive Committee and the Council of People's Commissars passed a decree on May 13, 1918, instituting food requisition (prodrazverstka), according to which peasants owed the state all surplus grain and other agriculture products that they did not require for sowing or personal sustenance. The government organized armed detachments of militants, who were soon roaming the countryside, confiscating what food they could find and shooting those who resisted. Thus began War Communism, a new, brutal phase of the Civil War. The crisis in agriculture intensified, but the Bolsheviks gathered enough food to support the Red Army. Lenin expounded on the food crisis and the forcible seizure of grain in the following telegram to the Congress of Soviets in the city of Penza. Is this Lenin at his most decisive, provisioning the army and crushing peasant opposition in one brutal stroke? Is he smashing the rural market economy on ideological impulse to institute a new order? Or is he improvising, a master tactician caught in a tough bind? Consider his six instructions to the Congress and decide.

The grain monopoly is being enforced simultaneously with a monopoly on textiles and on other staple articles of general consumption, and . . . the demand for the abolition of the grain monopoly is a political move

V. I. Lenin, *Collected Works*, vol. 27 (Moscow: Progress Publishers, 1964), 454–55.

on the part of counter-revolutionary strata, who are endeavoring to wrench from the hands of the revolutionary proletariat the system of monopoly regulation of prices, one of the most important implements for the general transition from capitalist exchange of commodities to socialist exchange of products. . . .

Point out that the only effective method of increasing bread rations is contained in the decision of the Council of People's Commissars to requisition grain forcibly from the kulaks and to distribute it among the poor of the cities and the countryside. This requires that the poor shall much more rapidly and resolutely enlist in the food army which is being created by the People's Commissariat for Food.

Propose that the Congress immediately start agitating among the workers to enlist in the food army formed by the Penza Soviet of Deputies and to abide by the following rules:

1) Every factory shall provide one person for every twenty-five of its workers.

2) Registration of those desiring to enlist in the food army shall be conducted by the factory committee, which shall draw up a list of the names of those mobilized, in two copies, one of which it shall deliver to the People's Commissariat for Food while retaining the other.

3) To the list must be attached a guarantee given by the factory committee, or by the trade union organization, or by a Soviet body, or by responsible representatives of Soviet organizations, testifying to the personal honesty and revolutionary discipline of every candidate. Members of the food army must be selected so that there will not in future be a single stain on the names of those who are setting out for the villages to combat the handful of predatory kulaks and save millions of toilers from starvation.

Comrades, workers, only if this condition is observed will it be obvious to all that the requisition of grain from the kulaks is not robbery but the fulfillment of a revolutionary duty to the worker and peasant masses who are fighting for socialism! . . .

6) Those enrolled in the army shall give a pledge that they will unreservedly carry out any instructions that may be given by the People's Commissariat for Food when the detachments leave for their place of operation, and that they will obey the commissars of the detachments.

36

From *Speech to the First All-Russian Congress of Land Departments, Poor Peasants' Committees, and Communes*

December 11, 1918

The Bolsheviks sought allies in the countryside as resistance mounted to their agricultural policies. They formed Poor Peasants' Committees of marginal peasants or sympathizers who were willing to help seize grain and other products. On November 21, 1918, the Council of People's Commissars issued a decree on the organization of supply that abolished the remnants of private trade. This policy became known as War Communism, *since it consigned to the state the distribution of all essential goods. Without being able to sell their grain, produce, or handicraft products in the market, peasants depended on the government for access to all goods except those that they produced themselves or could acquire by barter. Lenin and his colleagues, recognizing that the peasants had lost the incentive to grow more than they could consume, sought new forms of social organization to encourage production. To solve this problem, the Bolsheviks, and Lenin most of all, urged the creation of collective farms for poor peasants and for middling peasants who were willing to break with the existing rural order. Not surprisingly, the resulting farms fell into the hands of local officials, who managed them unproductively and corruptly.*

In the following speech, Lenin portrays peasants as a revolutionary force and divides village society, as he divided society in general, into unscrupulous overlords and oppressed underdogs.

The village was no longer united. The peasants, who had fought as one man against the landowners, now split into two camps—the camp of the more prosperous peasants and the camp of the poor peasants who, side by side with the workers, continued their steadfast advance toward

---

V. I. Lenin, *Collected Works*, vol. 28 (Moscow: Progress Publishers, 1965), 339–41, 343, 348.

socialism and changed from fighting the landowners to fighting capital, the power of money, and the use of the great land reform for the benefit of the kulaks. This struggle cut the property-owning and exploiting classes off from the revolution completely; it definitely put our revolution on the socialist road which the urban working class had tried so hard and vigorously to put it on in October, but along which it will not be able to direct the revolution successfully unless it finds firm, deliberate and solid support in the countryside.

There lies the significance of the revolution which took place this summer and autumn even in the most remote villages of Russia, a revolution which was not spectacular, not as striking and obvious as the October Revolution of last year, but whose significance is incomparably deeper and greater.

The formation of the Poor Peasants' Committees in the rural districts was the turning-point; it showed that the urban working class, which in October had united with all the peasants to crush the landowners, the principal enemy of the free, socialist Russia of the working people, had progressed from this to the much more difficult and historically more noble and truly socialist task—that of carrying the enlightening socialist struggle into the rural districts, and reaching the minds of the peasants as well. . . .

It goes without saying that a revolution of this kind, the transition from small individual peasant farms to collective farming, will take some time and can certainly not be accomplished at one stroke. . . .

The ruination left by the war simply does not allow us to restore the old small-scale peasant farms. Not only have the mass of the peasants been awakened by the war, not only has the war shown them what technical marvels now exist and how these marvels have been adapted for people's extermination, but it has also given rise to the idea that these technical marvels must be used primarily to reshape agriculture, the most common form of production in the country, in which the greatest number of people are engaged, but which at the same time is the most backward. . . .

In alliance with the urban workers and the socialist proletariat of the whole world, the working peasants of Russia can now be certain they will overcome all their adversaries, beat off all the attacks of the imperialists, and accomplish that without which the emancipation of the working people is impossible—collective farming, the gradual but steady transition from small individual farms to collective farming. (*Loud, prolonged applause.*)

37

From *Political Report of the Central Committee to the Eighth All-Russian Conference of the RCP(B)*

December 2, 1919

Lenin had sketched out only a vague economic strategy in 1918, and the concessions and exceptions authorized by the government prevented its realization.[28] Yet as the Civil War intensified and the economic situation worsened, he and other leaders adopted increasingly coercive methods. Trotsky speculated about "labor armies" in 1920 with Lenin's approval, and Lenin himself began to treat militarization as the basis of all administration, as in the following report.

This policy of ours as expressed in matters military must become the policy of our internal development. . . .

The bread problem. We have achieved much with our requisitioning system. Our food policy has made it possible in the second year to acquire three times as much grain as in the first. During three months of the last campaign more grain was produced than during three months of last year, although, as you will hear in the report by the People's Commissar for Food, it was accompanied by what were, without doubt, great difficulties. One raid by Mamontov[29] that took in the whole southern part of the central agricultural zone cost us very dear. But we have learned to carry out the requisitioning system, i.e., we have learned to make the peasants sell their grain to the state at fixed prices, without an equivalent in exchange. We know full well, of course, that paper money is not the equivalent of grain. We know that the peasant is loaning us his grain, and we ask him, "Should you hold back your grain waiting for an equivalent so that the workers can die of starvation? Do you want to trade on a free market and take us

[28]S.V. Kuleshov, ed., *Nashe Otechestvo: Opyt Politicheskoi Istorii*, vol. 2 (Moscow: Terra, 1991), 58.
[29]Konstantin Konstantinovich Mamontov (1869–1920), a Russian general and commander of the cavalry corps in the Voluntary Army in 1919.

V. I. Lenin, *Collected Works*, vol. 30 (Moscow: Progress Publishers, 1965), 182–84.

thereby back to capitalism?" Many intellectuals who have read Marx do not understand that freedom to trade is a return to capitalism; the peasant, however, understands it more easily. He knows that to sell bread at free prices, when the starving are prepared to pay anything for it, are prepared to give up all they have to escape death from starvation—he knows that this is a return to exploitation, that it is freedom for the rich to make a profit and ruination for the poor. We say that this is a crime against the state and we shall not yield an inch in this struggle. . . .

The requisitioning of grain must be the basis of all our activity. The food problem is at the basis of all problems. We have to devote a great deal of effort to defeat Denikin. There must not be the slightest hesitation or carelessness until the victory is complete, for all sorts of turns are possible. Whenever there is the slightest improvement in the war situation, however, we must devote greater effort to the work of food supplies because that is the basis of everything. The requisitioning must be carried out in full. Only when we have solved that problem shall we have a socialist foundation, and on that socialist foundation we shall be able to erect the splendid edifice of socialism that we have so often begun to build from the top and which has so often collapsed.

3

Threats to the Revolution: The Development of the New Economic Policy

In late 1920, with the end of the Civil War in sight, the Bolsheviks faced an exasperating economic and political situation. The Civil War and the policy of War Communism had exhausted the country. Most peasants as well as the industrial workers on whom Lenin and the Bolsheviks counted for support recoiled from the government and its economic experiments. The country exploded in large-scale rural rebellions, strikes, industrial disturbances, and mutinies, of which the most threatening was that of sailors at Petrograd's Kronstadt naval base.

There were also arguments and clashes inside the ruling party itself during the end of 1920 and the beginning of 1921. Several opposition groups, particularly the Democratic Centralists and the Workers' Opposition, challenged Lenin's leadership. The Workers' Opposition constituted the most serious threat since they demanded an independent role in government for trade unions as the workers' advocates. Disagreements among top party leaders intensified in the last months of 1920, and Lenin agreed to an open discussion at the session of the Party Central Committee on December 24. The discussion ranged over all the principal issues of the country's future.

The next day Trotsky, in his article "The Role and Tasks of the Trade Unions," raised questions about economic development, the management of the economy, social rights, administrative centralization, and democracy. A discussion began at the meeting of the Bolsheviks attending the Eighth Congress of Soviets on December 30, 1920. Lenin, with the support of Zinoviev, then a candidate member of the Central Committee, opposed Trotsky's proposals for using army units in industry and transportation and integrating trade unions into the state machine (*ogosudarstvlivaniie profsoiusov*). Lenin took a more moderate stance. Although the idea of the New Economic Policy had not yet ripened in his political thinking, he rejected proposals for the full militarization of labor. With an eye on the dissatisfied workers, he also rejected the idea of making trade unions state institutions, although in fact he was very close to Trotsky's view of them as "transmission belts" to carry out the party-government's policies.

Disputes and Opposition in the Party, 1920–1921

38

From *The Party Crisis*

January 21 (February 3), 1921

On January 14, 1921, Lenin and other members of the Central Committee signed the draft of the resolution that they wished to propose to the upcoming Tenth Party Congress. The draft, which concerned trade unions, became known as "The Platform of the Ten." In reply, the Workers' Opposition and the Democratic Centralists produced a platform of their own, in which they sought a role for workers in the management of industry and state administration. They also urged a partial democratization of the party. During the trade-union discussion, Trotsky aptly noted that Lenin's defense of trade unions was largely rhetorical. Lenin expressed his view of the "party crisis" in an article with that title in Pravda *on January 21, 1921. His position is remarkable for his denial of the right of Trotsky and others to discuss openly the party's problems, for his denunciation of opponents for forming a "faction," and for his refusal to make any concession to trade union independence. He condemns the Workers' Opposition as "syndicalist," referring to activists who thought trade unions should lead the anticapitalist struggle. Reading this document raises the question: Who, under these rules, could challenge the party elite's hegemony over society?*

V. I. Lenin, *Collected Works*, vol. 32 (Moscow: Progress Publishers, 1965), 43–44, 52–53.

The pre-Congress discussion is in full swing. Minor differences and disagreements have grown into big ones, which always happens when someone persists in a minor mistake and balks at its correction, or when those who are making a big mistake seize on the minor mistake of one or more persons.

That is how disagreements and splits always grow. That is how we "grew up" from minor disagreements to syndicalism [trade unionism], which means a complete break with communism and an inevitable split in the Party if it is not healthy and strong enough to purge itself of the malaise.

We must have the courage to face the bitter truth. The Party is sick. The Party is down with the fever. The whole point is whether the malaise has affected only the "feverish upper ranks," and perhaps only those in Moscow, or the whole organism. And if the latter is the case, is it capable of healing itself completely within the next few weeks, before the Party Congress and at the Party Congress, making a relapse impossible, or will the malaise linger and become dangerous?

What is it that needs to be done for a rapid and certain cure? *All* members of the Party must make a calm and painstaking *study* of 1) the essence of the disagreements and 2) the developments of the Party struggle. A study must be made by both, because the essence of the disagreements is revealed, clarified and specified (and very often transformed as well) in the *course of the struggle*, which, passing through its various stages, always shows, at every stage, a *different* line-up and number of combatants, *different* positions in the struggle, etc. A *study* must be made of both, and a demand made for the most exact, printed documents that can be thoroughly verified. Only a hopeless idiot will believe oral statements. If *no* documents are available, there must be an examination of witnesses on *both* or several sides and the grilling must take place in the presence of witnesses. . . .

Our platform up to now has been: Do not defend but rectify the bureaucratic excesses. The fight against bureaucracy is a long and arduous one. Excesses can and must be rectified at once. It is not those who point out harmful excesses and strive to rectify them but those who resist rectification that undermine the prestige of the military workers and appointees. Such were the excesses of certain Tsektranites[1] who, however, will continue to be (and have been) valuable

---

[1] Abbreviation for members of the Central Committee of the Trade Union of Transport Workers.

workers. There is no need to harass the trade unions by inventing dis-agreements with them, when they themselves have decided upon and accepted all that is new, business-like and practical in the tasks of the trade unions in production. On this basis, let us vigorously work together for practical results.

We have now added to our platform the following: We must combat the ideological discord and the *unsound* elements of the opposition who talk themselves into repudiating all "militarization of industry," and not only the "appointments method," which has been the prevailing one up to now, but all "appointments," that is, in the last analysis, repudiating the *Party's* leading role in relation to the non-Party masses. We must combat the syndicalist deviation, which will kill the Party unless it is entirely cured of it.

The Entente capitalists will surely try to take advantage of our Party's malaise to mount another invasion, and the Socialist-Revolutionaries, to hatch plots and rebellions. We need have no fear of this because we shall unite as one man, without being afraid to admit the malaise, but recognizing that it demands from all of us a greater discipline, tenacity and firmness at every post. By the time the Tenth Congress of the R.C.P. meets in March, and after the Congress, the Party will not be weaker, but stronger.

39

Summary of Lenin's Remarks at the Conference of the Delegates to the Tenth Congress of the RCP(B) — Supporters of the Platform of Ten

March 13, 1921

The results of the "trade union discussion" were summed up by the Tenth Congress of the RCP(B), which supported Lenin wholly. Although Lenin secured the acceptance at the Congress of his resolution "On Party Unity," which banished factions, he had to create his own faction to do

Richard Pipes, ed., *The Unknown Lenin: From the Secret Archive* (New Haven, Conn., and London: Yale University Press, 1996), 123–24.

so. The issues raised by the following document, the rough notes on his speech "Supporters of the Platform of Ten" (the full text was not preserved),[2] include his attitude toward opposition in the party, his willingness to discuss issues openly, and his view of Trotsky. The speech is also interesting for Lenin's list of dislikes, including the apparatus (the bureaucracy); the rebellious Kronstadt sailors, whom he accuses of anarchism; and various groups who sought more democracy in the party (Democratic Centralists) or a greater role for trade unions (Workers' Opposition).

Is the majority entitled to be a majority [?]. If it wants to be, then how should it be done [?]. For example, [of] three hundred, two hundred are the majority, and one hundred the minority. There arises the question of a split. A union is possible.

If the majority does not come to an arrangement, then the minority can win. This does happen. We are not a faction. We came as a faction, but we do not constitute a faction here. We should use our right in elections. In elections of delegates we have fought to win at the congress. And this we should do.

When the discussion got under way, then all saw the political mistake, and rightly so. It was a most dangerous discussion. The masses have taken it up, so they, too, have disagreements.

We must be firm, hard. Those who hesitate will join us.

Now as to Kronstadt. The danger there lies in the fact that their slogans are not Socialist Revolutionary, but anarchistic.

An All-Russian Congress of Producers[3]—this is not a Marxist but a petty bourgeois idea.

If you wish to introduce the opposition into the Central Committee to further its disintegration, then permit us not to permit it.

The "Workers' Opposition" expresses the vacillations of the non-party masses.

The "Democratic Center"[4] exists only in Moscow and unites only the intelligentsia. But it hinders work.

---

[2]Lenin's speech was recorded by I. N. Barakhov, who was the delegate from the Yakut party organization. Barakhov gave his manuscript to the Party Archive in 1929.

[3]The idea of an All-Russian Congress of Producers influenced anti-Bolshevik circles during the first years after the October Revolution. Some activists used it to try to circumvent the dictatorship's rules and elicit the grievances of workers and other strata of the population.

[4]Lenin had in mind the Group of Democratic Centralism.

Moscow is the best city in the sense that it has a mass of intelligentsia, creators of theses, ex-officials, etc.

I have been accused: ["]You are a son of a bitch for letting the discussion get out of hand.["] Well, try to stop Trotsky. How many divisions does one have to send against him?

The organization [*apparat*] is bad. Everyone hates the *glavki*.[5] But no one agrees to disperse them. It is politics for the organization, not the organization . . .

Our policy. From the point of view of the interests of the vanguard to the rear guard, of the whole class toward the peasantry [*sic*].

Yesterday about trade unions, and today to revamp the whole [military] command staff. Where are we to get the commissars [?].

We will come to terms with Trotsky.

The apparatus is for politics, not politics for the apparatus.

Trotsky wants to resign. Over the past three years I have had a lot of resignations in my pockets. And I have let some of them just lie there in store. But Trotsky is a temperamental man with military experience. He is in love with the organization, but as for politics, he hasn't got a clue.

40

From *Preliminary Draft Resolution of the Tenth Congress of the RCP on Party Unity*
March 1921

The most important resolution Lenin prepared for the Congress was "On Party Unity." Warning of enemies at every turn, he affirms the hierarchical nature of the party, denounces all breaches of discipline, impugns the motives of his critics, and threatens with expulsion all who challenge him and the party elite. He also reiterates the official (and untrue) assertion that the rebellious Kronstadt sailors were led by "white guards."

[5]Glavki (*glavnyie upravleniia*) were parts of the Supreme Council of the National Economy for different branches of industry and other economic spheres.

V. I. Lenin, *Collected Works*, vol. 32 (Moscow: Progress Publishers, 1965), 241, 243–44.

1. The Congress calls the attention of all members of the Party to the fact that the unity and cohesion of the ranks of the Party, the guarantee of complete mutual confidence among Party members and genuine team-work that really embodies the unanimity of will of the vanguard of the proletariat, are particularly essential at the present time, when a number of circumstances are increasing the vacillation among the petty-bourgeois population of the country.

2. Notwithstanding this, even before the general Party discussion on the trade unions, certain signs of factionalism had been apparent in the Party—the formation of groups with separate platforms, striving to a certain degree to segregate and create their own group discipline. Such symptoms of factionalism were manifested, for example, at a Party conference in Moscow (November 1920) and at a Party conference in Kharkov[6] by the so-called Workers' Opposition group, and partly by the so-called Democratic Centralism group.

All class-conscious workers must clearly realize that factionalism of any kind is harmful and impermissible, for no matter how members of individual groups may desire to safeguard Party unity, factionalism in practice inevitably leads to the weakening of team-work and to intensified and repeated attempts by the enemies of the governing Party, who have wormed their way into it, to widen the cleavage and to use it for counter-revolutionary purposes. . . .

4. In the practical struggle against factionalism, every organization of the Party must take strict measures to prevent all factional actions. Criticism of the Party's shortcomings, which is absolutely necessary, must be conducted in such a way that every practical proposal shall be submitted immediately, without any delay, in the most precise form possible, for consideration and decision to the leading local and central bodies of the Party. Moreover, every critic must see to it that the form of his criticism takes account of the position of the Party, surrounded as it is by a ring of enemies, and that the content of his criticism is such that, by directly participating in Soviet and Party work, he can test the rectification of the errors of the Party or of individual Party members in practice. Analyses of the Party's general line, estimates of its practical experience, check-ups of the fulfillment of its decisions, studies of methods of rectifying errors, etc., must under no circumstances be submitted for preliminary discussion to groups formed on the basis of "platforms," etc., but must in all cases be submitted for

[6]The Fifth All-Ukrainian Party Conference was held in Kharkov in November 1920. More than half of the delegates voted for the platform of the Workers' Opposition.

discussion directly to all the members of the Party. For this purpose, the Congress orders a more regular publication of *Diskussinny Listok*[7] and special symposiums to promote unceasing efforts to ensure that criticism shall be concentrated on essential and shall not assume a form capable of assisting the class enemies of the proletariat.

5. Rejecting in principle the deviation towards syndicalism and anarchism, which is examined in a special resolution,[8] and instructing the Central Committee to secure the complete elimination of all factionalism, the Congress at the same time declares that every practical proposal concerning questions to which the so-called Workers' Opposition group, for example, has devoted special attention, such as purging the Party of non-proletarian and unreliable elements, combating bureaucratic practices, developing democracy and workers' initiative, etc., must be examined with the greatest care and tested in practice. The Party must know that we have not taken all the necessary measures in regard to these questions because of various obstacles, but that, while ruthlessly rejecting impractical and factional pseudo-criticism, the Party will unceasingly continue—trying out new methods—to fight with all the means at its disposal against the evils of bureaucracy, for the extension of democracy and initiative, for detecting, exposing and expelling from the Party elements that have wormed their way into its rank, etc.

6. The Congress, therefore, hereby declares dissolved and orders the immediate dissolution of all groups without exception formed on the basis of one platform or another (such as the Workers' Opposition group, the Democratic Centralism group, etc.). Non-observance of this decision of the Congress shall entail unconditional and instant expulsion from the Party.

7. In order to ensure strict discipline within the Party and in all Soviet work and to secure the maximum unanimity in eliminating all factionalism, the Congress authorizes the Central Committee, in cases of breach of discipline or of a revival or toleration of factionalism, to apply all Party penalties, including expulsion, and in regard to members of the Central Committee, reduction to the status of alternative members and, as an extreme measure, expulsion from the Party. A

---

[7]*Diskussionny Listok* (Discussion Bulletin) was a non-periodical publication of the Central Committee of the party. Two issues came out before the Tenth Congress.

[8]The resolution "On the Syndicalist and Anarchist Deviation in Our Party" was adopted by the Tenth Congress. For the draft resolution, see V. I. Lenin, *Collected Works*, vol. 32 (Moscow: Progress Publishers, 1965), 245–48.

necessary condition for the application of such an extreme measure to members of the Central Committee, alternate members of the Central Committee and members of the Control Commission is the convocation of a Plenary Meeting of the Central Committee, to which all alternate members of the Central Committee and all members of the Control Commission shall be invited. If such a general assembly of the most responsible leaders of the Party deems it necessary by a two-thirds majority to reduce a member of the Central Committee to the status of alternate member, or to expel him from the Party, this measure shall be put into effect immediately.

Anti-Bolshevik Popular Uprisings and the Shift in Policy

After defeating the Whites and their foreign supporters, the Bolsheviks faced a threatening internal political crisis in late 1920 and early 1921. How Lenin responded shaped Soviet economic and social life for half a decade and Soviet political culture for the entire life of the Soviet regime. The magnitude of the crisis led him simultaneously to implement the "New Economic Policy," which opened the economy to market forces, while reinforcing his personal power and that of his circle within the party. Thus, in the last year of his active life, Lenin left the ambiguous legacy of a vaguely defined mixed economy in a dictatorial one-party state.

41

From *Report on the Political Work of the Central Committee of the RCP(B) on Tenth Congress of the RCP(B)*

March 8, 1921

The circumstances that led Lenin to adopt the New Economic Policy and strengthen his control were compelling. Victory in the Civil War had come at a high price. Having disposed of all organized opposition, the Bolsheviks faced a surge of spontaneous and violent popular hostility. The draconian measures of War Communism and political repression lost them much of the support they had gained in the first wave of revolutionary enthusiasm. Peasants had opposed War Communism from the outset, but in late 1920 and early 1921 they rebelled in Western Siberia, Central Asia, the Volga region, the provinces of Tambov and Voronezh, the Kuban', the Don region, and parts of Ukraine: that is, in most of the country. Shortages of food and consumer goods provoked anger and distress in the cities as well. Yet despite the danger of widespread famine, the government blockaded roads into Moscow, Petrograd, and other cities with detachments of soldiers to prevent peasants from trading with urban inhabitants desperate to barter possessions for food. The effect was to keep food from the hungry and to discourage peasants from producing a surplus.

The workers in whose name Lenin had seized power turned against him in response to layoffs at closed enterprises and the Bolshevik's dictatorial management of the surviving factories and plants in violation of earlier guarantees of workers' control. Strikes and disturbances spread through Petrograd factories during the second half of February 1920. In early March, sailors at the fortress of Kronstadt on the island of Kotlin in the Bay of Finland rose up, threatening the very existence of the Bolshevik regime. Rebellious sailors created a Temporary Revolutionary Committee under a clerk from the battleship Peropavlovsk, S. M. Petrichenko. *They affirmed their support for the revolution, but demanded an end to the Bolsheviks' economic dictatorship and monopoly on political power. They offered to negotiate, but Lenin and his government*

V. I. Lenin, *Collected Works*, vol. 32 (Moscow: Progress Publishers, 1965), 183–85.

refused. Bolshevik leaders used the fact that a former tsarist officer, Major-General A. N. Kozlovsky, chief artillery officer at the fortress from the end of 1920, had joined the rebels to denounce the uprising as a "conspiracy of White generals." The Red Army and other military units stormed the fortress on March 8 and exacted a bloody retribution. In the aftermath, over two thousand people were shot, and nearly seven thousand others were sentenced to various terms of imprisonment by special tribunals. The following document reveals Lenin's reasoning in response to the crisis and his manner of dismissing the widespread opposition to his rule.

I should now like to deal with the Kronstadt events. I have not yet received the latest news from Kronstadt, but I have no doubt that this mutiny, which very quickly revealed to us the familiar figures of white-guard generals, will be put down within the next few days, if not hours. There can be no doubt about this. But it is essential that we make a thorough appraisal of the political and economic lessons of this event.

What does it mean? It was an attempt to seize political power from the Bolsheviks by a motley crowd or alliance of ill-assorted elements, apparently just to the right of the Bolsheviks, or perhaps even to their "left"—you can't really tell, so amorphous is the combination of political groupings that has tried to take power in Kronstadt. You all know, undoubtedly, that at the same time whiteguard generals were very active over there. There is ample proof of this. A fortnight before the Kronstadt events, the Paris newspapers reported a mutiny at Kronstadt. It is quite clear that it is the work of Socialist-Revolutionaries and whiteguard émigrés, and at the same time the movement was reduced to a petty-bourgeois counter-revolution and petty-bourgeois anarchism. That is something quite new. This circumstance, in the context of all the crises, must be given careful political consideration and must be very thoroughly analyzed. There is evidence here of the activity of petty-bourgeois anarchist elements with their slogans of unrestricted trade and invariable hostility to the dictatorship of the proletariat. This mood has had a wide influence on the proletariat. It has an effect on factories in Moscow and a number of provincial centers. This petty-bourgeois counter-revolution is undoubtedly more dangerous than Denikin, Yudenich and Kolchak put together, because ours is a country where the proletariat is in a minority, where peasant property has gone to ruin and where, in addition, the demobilization has set loose vast numbers of potentially mutinous elements. No matter how big or small the initial, shall I say, shift in power, which the Kronstadt sailors and workers put forward—they wanted to correct the Bolsheviks in regard to restrictions in trade—and this looks like a small shift, which leaves the same slogans of "Soviet power" with ever so slight a change or correction. Yet, in actual fact the whiteguards only used the non-Party elements as a stepping stone to get in. This is politically inevitable. We saw the petty bourgeois, anarchist elements in the Russian revolution, and we have been fighting them for decades. We have seen them in action since February 1917, during the great revolution, and their parties' attempts to prove that their program differed little from that of the Bolsheviks, but that only their methods in carrying it through were different. We know this not only from the experience of the October Revolution, but also of the outlying regions and various areas within the former Russian Empire where the Soviet power was temporarily replaced by other regimes. Let us recall the Democratic Committee in Samara.[9] They all came in demanding equality, freedom, and a constituent assembly, and every time they proved to be nothing but a conduit for whiteguard rule.

42

Rough Draft of Theses Concerning the Peasants
February 8, 1921

As early as February 1921, Lenin began to see that the dangers threatening the Bolshevik regime were the result of War Communism. His first indication of the need for change was cautious. At a conference of metalworkers on February 4, 1921, he hinted at the need to reestablish economic relations between workers and peasants. "We are not opposed to

[9]In June 1918, after Samara was captured by the mutinous Czechoslovakian army corps, a Committee of the Members of the Constituent Assembly (Komuch) was formed of Mensheviks, SRs, and members of other parties. The Komuch ceased to exist after the Red Army occupied the Volga and Ural regions in the fall of the same year.

V. I. Lenin, *Collected Works*, vol. 32 (Moscow: Progress Publishers, 1965), 133.

*reviving these relations," he noted, implying a return to some form of
market link between city and countryside.*[10] *Thus at this stage he still
wavered between War Communism and some sort of compromise. On
February 8, he drafted his theses about discontent among the peasants.
Lenin's main idea was to replace the forcible seizure of peasant stocks
with a tax in kind to encourage the peasants to produce a surplus that
could be exchanged for consumer goods. He did not envisage a free market for agricultural products.*

1. Satisfy the wish of the non-Party peasants for the substitution of a tax in kind for the surplus appropriation system (the confiscation of surplus grain stocks).

2. Reduce the size of this tax as compared with last year's appropriation rate.

3. Approve the principle of making the tax commensurate with the farmer's effort, reducing the rate for those making the greater effort.

4. Give the farmer more leeway in using his after-tax surpluses in local trade, provided his tax is promptly paid up in full.

Lenin's Objective in the New Economic Policy

43

From *Report on the Substitution of a Tax in Kind for the Surplus Grain Appropriation System*
March 15, 1921

Lenin's view of the NEP is critical for evaluating his role in the formation of the Soviet Union. If he sought a mixed economy extending over many years, then the Soviet command economy, in which the state decided how resources should be allocated and acted as almost the only

[10]V. I. Lenin, *Collected Works*, vol. 32, 110.

V. I. Lenin, *Collected Works*, vol. 32 (Moscow: Progress Publishers, 1965), 214–19.

employer, was hardly Lenin's legacy. Yet if he sought merely a brief respite before further expanding the state's economic power, then he is perhaps its true founder. In the following report, which he presented only after his unanimous approval as party leader in the election of the Central Committee at the Tenth Party Congress, he treats the NEP as a political compromise involving considerable risk. Lenin expressed different views of the NEP, however, at different times.

Comrades, the question of substituting a tax for surplus-grain appropriation is primarily and mainly a political question, for it is essentially a question of the attitude of the working class to the peasantry. We are raising it because we must subject the relations of these two main classes, whose struggle or agreement determines the fate of our revolution as a whole, to a new or, I should perhaps say, a more careful and correct re-examination and some revision. There is no need for me to dwell in detail on the reasons for it. You all know very well of course what totality of causes, especially those due to the extreme want arising out of the war, ruin, demobilization, and the disastrous crop failure—you know about the totality of circumstances that has made the condition of the peasantry especially precarious and critical and was bound to increase its swing from the proletariat to the bourgeoisie. . . .

We know that so long as there is no revolution in other countries, only agreement with the peasantry can save the socialist revolution in Russia. And that is how it must be stated, frankly, at all meetings and in the entire press. We know that the agreement between the working class and the peasantry is not solid—to put it mildly, without entering the word "mildly" in the minutes—but, speaking plainly it is very much worse. Under no circumstances must we try to hide anything; we must plainly state that the peasantry is dissatisfied with the form of our relations, that it does not want relations of this type and will not continue to live as it has hitherto. This is unquestionable. The peasantry has expressed its will in this respect definitely enough. It is the will of the vast masses of the working population. We must reckon with this, and we are sober enough politicians to say frankly: let us re-examine our policy in regard to the peasantry. The state of affairs that has prevailed so far cannot be continued any longer.

We must say to the peasants: "If you want to turn back, if you want to restore private property and unrestricted trade in their entirely, it will certainly and inevitably mean falling under the rule of the landowners and the capitalists. This has been proved by a number of examples from history and examples of revolutions. The briefest examination of the ABC of communism and political economy will prove that this is inevitable. Let us then look into the matter. Is it or is it not in the interest of the peasantry to part ways with the proletariat only to slip back—and let the country slip back—to the rule of the capitalists and landowners? Consider this, and let us consider it together."

We believe that if the matter is given proper consideration, the conclusion will be in our favor, in spite of the admittedly deep gulf between the economic interests of the proletariat and the small farmer.

Difficult as our position is in regard to resources, the needs of the middle peasantry must be satisfied. There are far more middle peasants now than before, the antagonisms have been smothered out, the land has been distributed for use far more equally, the kulak's[11] position has been undermined and he has been in considerable measure expropriated—in Russia more than in the Ukraine, and less in Siberia. On the whole, however, statistics show quite definitely that there has been a leveling out, equalization, in the village, that is, the old sharp division into kulaks and cropless peasants has disappeared. Everything has become more equable, the peasantry in general has acquired the status of the middle peasant. . . .

We must try to satisfy the demands of the peasants who are dissatisfied and disgruntled, and legitimately so, and who cannot be otherwise. We must say to them: "Yes, this cannot go on any longer." How is the peasant to be satisfied and what does satisfying him mean? Where is the answer? Naturally it lies in the demands of the peasantry. We know these demands. But we must verify them and examine all that we know of the farmer's economic science. If we go into this, we shall see at once that it will take essentially two things to satisfy the small farmer. The first is a certain freedom of exchange, freedom for the small private proprietor, and the second is the need to obtain commodities and products. What indeed would free exchange amount to if there was nothing to exchange, and freedom of trade, if there was nothing to trade with! It would all remain on paper, and classes cannot be satisfied with scraps of paper, they want the goods. These two conditions must be clearly understood. The second—how to get

---

[11]*Kulak* is also a denigrating term for a country dweller. It previously had many meanings including rich peasant, usurer, profiteer, etc. In Bolshevik parlance, a kulak was a rich man who exploited poor peasants.

commodities and whether we shall be able to obtain them—we shall discuss later. It is the first condition—free exchange—that we must deal with now.

What is free exchange? It is unrestricted trade, and that means turning back toward capitalism. Free exchange and freedom of trade mean circulation of commodities between petty proprietors. All of us who have studied at least the elements of Marxism know that this exchange and freedom of trade inevitably lead to a division of commodity producers into owners of capital and owners of labor-power, a division into capitalists and wage-workers, i.e., a revival of capitalist wage-slavery, which does not fall from the sky but springs the world over precisely from the agricultural commodity economy. This we know perfectly well in theory, and anyone in Russia who has observed the small farmer's life and the conditions under which he farms must have seen this.

How then can the Communist Party recognize freedom to trade and accept it? Does not the proposition contain irreconcilable contradictions? The answer is that the practical solution of the problem naturally presents exceedingly great difficulties. I can foresee, and I know from the talks I have had with some comrades, that the preliminary draft on replacing surplus-grain appropriation by a tax—it has been handed out to you—gives rise to legitimate and inevitable questions, mostly as regards permitting exchange of goods within the framework of local economic turnover. This is set forth at the end of Point 8. What does it mean, what limits are there to this exchange, how is it all to be implemented? Anyone who expects to get the answer at the Congress will be disappointed. We shall find the answer in our legislation; it is our task to lay down the principle to be followed and provide the slogan. Our Party is the government party and the decision the Party Congress passes will be obligatory for the entire Republic: it is now up to us to decide the question in principle. We must do this and inform the peasantry of our decision, for the sowing season is almost at hand. Further we must muster our whole administrative apparatus, all our theoretical forces and all our practical experience, in order to see how it can be done. Can it be done at all, theoretically speaking: can freedom of trade, freedom of capitalist enterprise for the small farmer, be restored to a certain extent without undermining the political power of the proletariat? Can it be done? Yes, it can, for everything hinges on the extent. If we were able to obtain even a small quantity of goods and hold them in the hands of the state—the proletariat exercising political power—and if we could release these goods into circulation, we, as the state, would add economic power to our political power. Release of these goods into circulation would stimulate small farming, which is in a terrible state and cannot develop owing to the grievous war conditions and the economic chaos. The small farmer, so long as he remains small, needs a spur, an incentive that accords with his economic basis, i.e., the individual small farm. Here you cannot avoid local free exchange. If this turnover gives the state, in exchange for manufactured goods, a certain minimum amount of grain to cover urban and industrial requirements, economic circulation will be revived, with state power remaining in the hands of the proletariat and growing stronger. The peasants want to be shown in practice that the worker who controls the mills and factories—industry—is capable of organizing exchange with the peasantry. And, on the other hand, the vastness of our agricultural country with its poor transport system, boundless expanses, varying climate, diverse farming conditions, etc., makes a certain freedom of exchange between local agriculture and local industry, on a local scale, inevitable. In this respect, we are very much to blame for having gone too far; we overdid the nationalization of industry and trade, clamping down on local exchange of commodities. Was that a mistake? It certainly was.

44

Draft Resolution on the Question of the New Economic Policy for the Tenth Conference of the RCP(B)

May 1921

Lenin's proposals for economic reform were still vague in the spring of 1921. This is understandable since rank-and-file party members were not yet ready for radical measures. The party congress accepted Lenin's proposals, but this was only the beginning of the New Economic Policy, which developed gradually in reaction to the disintegrating economy and popular pressure for reform. The Tenth Party Conference, in May 1921,

V. I. Lenin, *Collected Works*, vol. 32 (Moscow: Progress Publishers, 1965), 433–35.

witnessed a new phase in the Bolsheviks' efforts to surmount Russia's economic crisis. The title of Lenin's report was the same as that of his remarks at the Tenth Party Congress in March on the tax in kind, but the resolution for the conference contained an additional section, "On Questions of the New Economic Policy." In this resolution, which the conference accepted, the NEP was expected to last "for a long period of years," and commodity exchange was expected to function both locally and more widely, through state-supported small and medium private and cooperative enterprises, and then by other means. Lenin, however, personally remained deeply ambivalent about the market. He did not introduce free trade in grain and other foodstuffs in this resolution. He allowed peasants to barter their surpluses for state industrial and consumer goods only through cooperatives.[12]

---

1. The fundamental political task of the moment is for all Party and Soviet workers to gain a complete understanding of the New Economic Policy and to implement it to the letter.

The Party regards this policy as being established for a long period of years, and demands that everyone should carry it out unconditionally with thoroughness and diligence.

2. Commodity exchange is brought to the fore as the principal lever of the New Economic Policy. It is impossible to establish a correct relationship between the proletariat and the peasantry, or an altogether stable form of economic alliance between these two classes in the period of transition from capitalism to socialism, without regular commodity exchange or the exchange of products between industry and agriculture.

The exchange of commodities, in particular, is required to stimulate the extension of the peasants' area under crop and improvement of peasant farming.

Local initiative and enterprise must be given all-round support and development at all costs.

Gubernias[13] with the greatest grain surpluses must be placed on the priority list for commodity exchange.

---

[12]Maurice Dobb, *Soviet Economic Development since 1917* (London: International Publishers, 1948), 131; Richard Pipes, ed., *The Unknown Lenin: From the Secret Archive* (New Haven, Conn., and London: Yale University Press, 1996), 127.

[13]Gubernias were provinces in prerevolutionary Russia. At the end of the 1920s, they were changed into oblasts. During the Civil War and shortly after, there were also oblasts (regions) that included several gubernias.

3. Considering co-operatives to be the main apparatus for commodity exchange, the conference recognizes as correct the policy of contracts between the agencies of the People's Commissariat for Food Supply and the co-operative societies, and the transfer, under government control, by the former to the latter of commodity-exchange stocks to fulfill the assignments of the government;

the co-operatives to be given broad opportunities for procurement and all-round development of local industry and revival of economic life in general;

support for credit operations by the co-operatives;

anarchic commodity exchange (that is, exchange which eludes all control and state supervision) to be combated by concentration of exchange chiefly in the hands of the co-operatives, without, however, any restrictions on regular free market operations;

market analysis.

4. Support for small and medium (private and co-operative) enterprises, chiefly those not requiring supplies from state raw material, fuel and food reserves.

Permission to lease government enterprises to private persons, co-operatives, artels and associations. The right of local economic agencies to conclude such contracts without authorization from superior agencies. Obligatory notification of the Council of Labor and Defense in each such case.

5. Review of (certain sections of) production programmes for large-scale industry towards increasing the manufacture of consumer goods and peasant household articles.

Extension of enterprise and initiative by each large establishment in the disposal of financial and material resources. Submission of a precise decree to that effect for approval by the Council of People's Commissars.

6. Development of the system of bonuses in kind and the establishment by way of experiment of a collective supply system.

Establishment of a more correct distribution of foodstuffs with the aim of increasing labor productivity.

7. The need to maintain and enlarge the apparatus for the full and expeditious collection of the tax in kind everywhere. Investment of food agencies with the necessary Party authority for that purpose. Maintenance and enhancement of the centralization of the food apparatus.

8. To concentrate all the enumerated on the current year's practical and urgent task: collection of at least 400 million poods[14] of grain

---

[14]One pood equals roughly 16 kilograms.

stocks as a basis for the rehabilitation of large-scale industry and the implementation of the electrification plan.

9. To adopt in principle the draft Instructions of the C.L.D.,[15] authorizing the All-Russian Central Executive Committee group[16] to enact them into law.

To recognize the strict fulfillment of the Instructions in general and the recruitment and promotion of non-Party people for work, in particular, as the Party's unconditional and primary task.

10. To establish special responsibility on the part of central agencies for any hampering of local initiative and insufficient support of it. To authorize the All-Russian Central Executive Committee group to work out a corresponding decision and have it adopted at the very next session.

11. The conference authorizes the Central Committee and all Party organizations to carry out a system of measures to intensify agitation and propaganda and effect the necessary transfer of Party cadres to ensure complete understanding and steady implementation of the enumerated tasks.

12. To set as the Party's most important task the careful and all-round publicizing and study in the press and at trade union, Soviet, and Party meetings, conferences, congresses, etc., of the practical experience gained in economic development locally and at the center.

[15]The Council of Labor and Defense (CLD) of the RSFSR was the governmental body responsible for economic development and defense. CLD was created in 1920 as a result of the reorganization of the Council of Workers' and Peasants' Defense, which had acted as a commission of the Council of People's Commissars. The CLD of the USSR existed from 1923 until 1937.
[16]Lenin had in mind the Communist faction in the All-Russian Central Executive Committee.

45

V. I. LENIN AND V. M. MOLOTOV

Telegram to All Provincial and Regional Party Committees of the RCP(B)

July 30, 1921

Lenin was still trying to suppress free trade in food products as late as July 1921, as his and Molotov's statements reveal. Even the onset of famine did not dissuade him from the confiscation of grain. The following document shows him repeatedly affirming the need for coercive bureaucratic solutions to Russia's food crisis. In the staccato language of the telegram, Lenin invokes his vision of a gigantic apparatus of officials solving Russia's problems on his personal orders. At this time he still did not consider even a partial reliance on the market. Rather, as the telegram implies, this is something he would come to consider openly only after all other options had failed.

To All Provincial and Regional Committees:

In confirming the circular telegram to the provincial executive committees and the provincial food committees signed by Sovnarkom Chairman Lenin and Deputy People's Supply Commissar Briukhanov[17] under No. 251,[18] the Central Committee directs the attention of the provincial committees to the following: 1) the food situation of the republic is extremely difficult, owing to crop failures in a number of provinces. For a number of reasons, free trade and free barter do not solve the supply problems. A rise in prices for agricultural produce can be observed everywhere [along with] a relative drop in the prices

[17]Nikolai Pavlovich Briukhanov (1878–1942) was the deputy commissar of supply during the Civil War. Later, he became the people's commissar of finance.
[18]This telegram informed local bodies of the categorization of areas by their level of yield.

Richard Pipes, ed., *The Unknown Lenin: From the Secret Archive* (New Haven, Conn., and London: Yale University Press, 1996), 130–31.

of manufactured goods. 2) For this reason, at the present time one should not exaggerate the significance of commodity exchange and relegate [food] taxation to a second place, which would be criminal shortsightedness. The chief condition for resolving the food crisis lies in the successful collection of taxes in [the form of] food. In light of the above, the Central Committee categorically orders the provincial committees: 1) to take immediate steps to restore and strengthen the food [collecting] apparatus, safeguarding it throughout [each] province from dislocation [and] the turnover in food workers without the consent of the supply commissars and the Supply Commissariat; 2) to reinforce the food apparatus by means of additional mobilizations of party and professional forces in order to establish a tax inspection staff within two weeks without fail, with at least one person per district; 3) given the novelty of the matter and for the guidance of the village soviets, to provide at least one comrade per district as an interim inspector; 4) to organize [and] unfold extensive agitation [among] the rural population, explaining the economic benefit of timely and full payment of taxes; 5) to enlist rural Communist cells to assist the rural soviets in the collection of taxes; 6) to raise the authority of the food agencies in party and Soviet circles and among the population; [the agencies' reputation] has suffered greatly in the period of transition to the new [economic] policy, and measures should be taken to stop the indiscriminate, unfounded accusations against food workers; 7) to take steps to reinstate comrades engaged in food work whose guilt has not been proven; 8) not to lose sight of the fact that the successful collection of taxes, which are an obligation, is ensured by the right granted under the law to district and provincial supply commissars to levy judicial [or] administrative punishment on tax evaders, as well as the right to limit and even temporarily prohibit free barter; 9) to appoint to chairmanships of the supply sessions of Revolutionary Tribunals reliable comrades who have had a connection with food work in the past and who are familiar with it; 10) to establish full contact between food agencies and party organizations and also food agencies of executive committees, especially of the rural soviets and district executive committees; 11) to provide the food agencies with the necessary party authority and the total power of the state apparatus of coercion. The Central Committee [hereby] orders the provincial committees, along with the executive committees and provincial food committees, to inform the Central Committee at least once a week, with copies to the Supply Commissariat, on the progress of preparatory work and the implementation of these directives. Especially responsible comrades of the Central Committee and Supply Commissariat are to be appointed to monitor the information. Responsibility for the correct and timely preparation of the supply apparatus is placed personally on the secretaries and members of the provincial [party] committees, chairmen of the provincial executive committees, and the provincial supply commissars.

> Signed: Chairman of the Council of Labor
> and Defense, Comrade Lenin
> Central Committee Secretary,
> Molotov

46

From *The Political Report of the Central Committee of the RCP(B) to the Eleventh Congress of the RCP(B)*

March 27, 1922

Lenin and his colleagues distrusted the market as a feature of the New Economic Policy or, as he sometimes called it, "state capitalism": that is, capitalism controlled and managed by the state. The term state capitalism *was not entirely appropriate. Although the state retained the ownership of large-scale enterprises, mining, banks, foreign trade, and the "commanding heights" of the economy, as well as control over the whole economy, the market did function in a limited fashion, and private ownership was permitted in small and middle industry, domestic trade, and consumer services, that is, in enterprises such as barbershops, restaurants, and small shops.*

Lenin delivered the Central Committee's report summing up the results of the NEP at the Eleventh Party Congress in March 1922. He defended the policy as an essential step in overcoming Russian peasant capitalism, but promised it could be disposed of in the near future. When considering Lenin's legacy, it is useful to note his repeated use of the phrase

V. I. Lenin, *Collected Works*, vol. 33 (Moscow: Progress Publishers, 1965), 277–80, 285.

"ending of retreat" in the following excerpt from his report. Also, notice the other repetitions and inconsistencies in this document, which could well be a result of the deterioration of his health and mental condition.

We had many outlets and loopholes that enabled us to escape from our political and economic difficulties. We can proudly say that up to now we have been able to utilize these outlets and loopholes in various combinations corresponding to the varying circumstances. But now we have no other outlets. Permit me to say this to you without exaggeration, because in that respect it is really "the last and decisive battle," not against international capitalism—against that we shall yet have many "last and decisive battles"—but against Russian capitalism, against the capitalism that is growing out of the small-peasant economy, the capitalism that is fostered by the latter. Here we shall have a fight on our hands in the immediate future, and the date of it cannot be fixed exactly. Here the "last and decisive battle" is impending; here there are no political or any other flanking movements that we can undertake, because this is a test in competition with private capital. Either we pass this test in competition with private capital, or we fail completely. To help us pass it we have political power and a host of economic and other resources; we have everything you want except ability. We lack ability. And if we learn this simple lesson from the experience of last year and take it as our guiding line for the whole of 1922, we shall conquer this difficulty, too, in spite of the fact that it is much greater than the previous difficulty, for it rests upon ourselves. It is not like some external enemy. The difficulty is that we ourselves refuse to admit the unpleasant truth forced upon us; we refuse to undertake the unpleasant duty that the situation demands of us, namely, to start learning from the beginning. That, in my opinion, is the second lesson that we must learn from the New Economic Policy.[19]

The third, supplementary lesson is on the question of state capitalism. . . . On the question of state capitalism, I think that generally our press and our Party make the mistake of dropping into intellectualism, into liberalism; we philosophize about how state capitalism is to be interpreted, and look into old books. But in those old books you will

---

[19]The "first lesson," as Lenin put it, was that the Russian economy was subordinated to an inner and an international market, in which "we may be beaten economically and politically" (Lenin, *Collected Works*, vol. 33 [Moscow: Progress Publishers, 1965], 276–77).

not find what we are discussing; they deal with the state capitalism that exists under capitalism. Not a single book has been written about state capitalism under communism. It did not occur even to Marx to write a word on this subject; and he died without leaving a single precise statement of definite instruction on it. That is why we must overcome the difficulty entirely by ourselves. And if we make a general mental survey of our press and see what has been written about state capitalism, as I tried to do when I was preparing this report, we shall be convinced that it is missing the target, that it is looking in an entirely wrong direction. . . .

State capitalism is capitalism that we must confine within certain bounds; but we have not yet learned to confine it within those bounds. That is the whole point. And it rests with us to determine what this state capitalism is to be. We have sufficient, quite sufficient political power; we also have sufficient economic resources at our command, but the vanguard of the working class which has been brought to the forefront to directly supervise, to determine the boundaries, to demarcate, to subordinate and not be subordinated itself, lacks sufficient ability for it. And what is needed here is ability, and that is what we do not have.

Never before in history has there been a situation in which the proletariat, the revolutionary vanguard, possessed sufficient political power and had state capitalism existing alongside it. The whole question turns on our understanding that this is the capitalism that we can and must permit, that we can and must confine within certain bounds; for this capitalism is essential for the broad masses of the peasantry and for private capital, which must trade in such a way as to satisfy the needs of the peasantry. We must organize things in such a way as to make possible the customary operation of capitalist economy and capitalist exchange, because this is essential for the people. Without it, existence is impossible. . . .

Well, we have lived through a year, the state is in our hands; but has it operated the New Economic Policy in the way we wanted in this past year? No. But we refuse to admit that it did not operate in the way we wanted. How did it operate? The machine refused to obey the hand that guided it. It was like a car that was going not in the direction the driver desired, but in the direction someone else desired; as if it were being driven by some mysterious, lawless hand, God knows whose, perhaps of a profiteer, or of a private capitalist, or of both. Be that as it may, the car is not going quite in the direction the man at the wheel imagines, and often it goes in an altogether different direction. This is the main thing that must be remembered in regard to state capitalism. In this main field we must start learning from the very beginning, and only when we have thoroughly understood and appreciated this can we be sure that we shall learn.

Now I come to the question of halting the retreat, a question I dealt with in my speech at the Congress of Metalworkers. Since then I have not heard any objection, either in the Party press, or in private letters from comrades, or in the Central Committee. The Central Committee approved my plan, which was, that in the report of the Central Committee to the present Congress strong emphasis should be laid on calling a halt to this retreat and that the Congress should give binding instructions on behalf of the whole Party accordingly. For a year we have been retreating. On behalf of the Party we must now call a halt. The purpose pursued by the retreat has been achieved. This period is drawing, or has drawn, to a close. We now have a different objective, that of regrouping our forces. We have reached a new line; on the whole, we have conducted the retreat in fairly good order. True, not a few voices were heard from various sides, which tried to convert this retreat into a stampede. Some—for example, several members of the group which bore the name of Workers' Opposition (I don't think they had any right to that name)—argued that we were not retreating properly in some sector or other. Owing to their excessive zeal they found themselves at the wrong door, and now they realize it. At that time they did not see that their activities did not help us to correct our movement, but merely had the effect of spreading panic and hindering our effort to beat a disciplined retreat. . . .

The retreat is at an end. The principal methods of operation, of how we are to work with the capitalists, are outlined. We have examples, even if an insignificant number.

Stop philosophizing and arguing about NEP. Let the poets write verses, that is what they are poets for. But you economists, you stop arguing about NEP and get more companies formed; check up on how many Communists we have who can organize successful competition with the capitalists.

The retreat has come to an end; it is now a matter of regrouping our forces. These are the instructions that the Congress must pass so as to put an end to fuss and bustle. Calm down, do not philosophize; if you do, it will be counted as a black mark against you. Show by your practical efforts that you can work no less efficiently than the capitalists. The capitalists create an economic link with the peasants in order to amass wealth; you must create a link with peasant economy in order to strengthen the economic power of our proletarian state. You have the advantage over the capitalists in that political power is in your hands; you have a number of economic weapons at your command; the only trouble is that you cannot make proper use of them. Look at things more soberly. Cast off the tinsel, the festive communist garments learn a simple thing simply, and we shall beat the private capitalist. We possess political power; we possess a host of economic weapons. If we beat capitalism and create a link with peasant farming we shall become an absolutely invincible power. Then the building of socialism will not be the task of that drop in the ocean, called the Communist Party, but the task of the entire mass of the working people. Then the rank-and-file peasants will see that we are helping them and they will follow our lead. Consequently, even if the pace is a hundred times slower, it will be a million times more certain and more sure.

It is in this sense that we must speak of halting the retreat; and the proper thing to do is, in one way or another, to make this slogan a Congress decision.

Economic Policy under the NEP

47

From *Five Years of the Russian Revolution and the Prospects of the World Revolution: Report to the Fourth Congress of the Communist International*
November 13, 1922

Seven months after his report to the Eleventh Party Congress, Lenin summarized the results of the NEP in his address to the Communist International. Many changes had occurred in the interim. In May 1921, the fundamental law of War Communism, which provided for the nationalization

V. I. Lenin, *Collected Works*, vol. 33 (Moscow: Progress Publishers, 1965), 418–19, 421–22, 426–28.

of all enterprises in all branches of industry, was abandoned. Market relations revived, and many middle- and small-scale private enterprises began to function profitably. Some state enterprises were leased to foreign capitalists and economic groups as "concessions," with positive results. Lenin nevertheless continued to consider private owners and capitalists his mortal enemies. At the end of 1921, he broached the idea of making state enterprises self-supporting: that is, having them run on a commercial basis to compete with private firms.

Lenin and his colleagues also tried to contain the market as well as the capitalists whom he believed would always try to cheat the state. In September 1922, for example, on Lenin's initiative, the Politburo of the Central Committee introduced criminal and civil legislation to permit the immediate cancellation of all concessions if necessary. In addition, when some Soviet leaders suggested offering a concession that seemed beneficial for the Soviet economy to the British entrepreneur Lesly Urquhart, Lenin brusquely opposed it. G. E. Zinoviev recalled that Lenin justified himself with the observation, "It is better to have a slowly recovering Soviet Russia that is poor and gray but our own than a Soviet [Russia] that is recovering quickly as a result of letting such a goat as Urquart into the kitchen-garden."[20] The NEP helped preserve Bolshevik rule, but close governmental supervision quickly produced unwanted results, including the subversion of the local and even central economic administration by criminal elements, widespread corruption, bureaucracy, red tape, and other ills. Lenin summarized some of the results of the NEP in his report to the Fourth Congress of the Communist International (November 1922). As is apparent from the text, Lenin was eager to convince the foreign delegates that Russia was proceeding toward socialism and was therefore a model for other countries and communist parties, particularly in Europe. Although the positive economic effect was evident only after his death in 1924, Lenin could bask in the glow of success as he stood before the foreign delegates. The regime seemed secure, and he attributed this chiefly to the management of relations with the peasants. The Civil War was over, the mass rebellions crushed, and the Bolsheviks retained their unchallenged political monopoly, which they celebrated as the dictatorship of the proletariat. Neither foreign failures nor the famine that ravaged the country nor even the militants' reservations about the NEP could detract from Lenin's glory. He expressed his optimistic and self-congratulatory feelings in his report.

---

[20]S. V. Kuleshov, ed., et al. *Nashe Otechestvo: Opyt Politicheskoi Istorii,* vol. 2 (Moscow: Terra, 1991), 168.

(*Comrade Lenin is met with stormy, prolonged applause and a general ovation. All rise and join in singing "The Internationale."*)[21] Comrades, I am down in the list as the main speaker, but you will understand that after my lengthy illness[22] I am not able to make a long report. I can only make a few introductory remarks on the key questions. My subject will be a very limited one. The subject, "Five Years of the Russian Revolution and the Prospects of the World Revolution," is in general too broad and too large for one speaker to exhaust in a single speech. That is why I shall take only a small part of this subject, namely, the question of the New Economic Policy. I have deliberately taken only this small part in order to make you familiar with what is now the most important question—at all events, it is the most important to me, because I am now working on it.

And so, I shall tell you how we launched the New Economic Policy, and what results we have achieved with the aid of this policy. If I confine myself to this question, I shall, perhaps, succeed in giving you a general survey and a general idea of it.

To begin with how we arrived at the New Economic Policy, I must quote from an article I wrote in 1918.[23] At the beginning of 1918, in a brief polemic, I touched on the question of the attitude we should adopt towards state capitalism. I then wrote:

> State capitalism would be a *step forward* as compared with the present state of affairs (i.e., the state of affairs at that time) in our Soviet Republic. If in approximately six months' time state capitalism became established in our Republic, this would be a great success and a sure guarantee that within a year socialism will have gained a permanently firm hold and will have become invincible in our country.

Of course, this was said at a time when we were more foolish than we are now, but not so foolish as to be unable to deal with such matters. . . .

Now that I have emphasized the fact that as early as 1918 we regarded state capitalism as a possible line of retreat, I shall deal with the results of our New Economic Policy. I repeat: at that time it was

---

[21]This formula arose during Lenin's rule and is evidence that his cult was already well established. Editors also used this and similar devices to convey unanimity and enhance the power of the ruling elite.

[22]In May 1922, Lenin suffered a major stroke. After several months of intensive treatment, his health improved. He returned to work in October 1922, but with great limitations.

[23]Lenin had in mind the article "'Left-Wing' Childishness and the Petty-Bourgeois Mentality," published in V. I. Lenin, *Collected Works*, vol. 27 (Moscow: Progress Publishers, 1965), 323–54.

still a very vague idea, but in 1921, after we had passed through the most important stage of the Civil War—and passed through it victoriously—we felt the impact of a grave—I think it was the gravest—internal political crisis in Soviet Russia. This internal crisis brought to light discontent not only among a considerable section of the peasantry but also among the workers. This was the first and, I hope, the last time in the history of Soviet Russia that feeling ran against us among large masses of peasants, not consciously but instinctively. What gave rise to this peculiar, and for us, of course, very unpleasant, situation? The reason for it was that in our economic offensive we had run too far ahead, that we had not provided ourselves with adequate resources, that the masses sensed what we ourselves were not then able to formulate consciously but what we admitted soon after, a few weeks later, namely, that the direct transition to purely socialist forms, to purely socialist distribution, was beyond our available strength, and that if we were unable to effect a retreat so as to confine ourselves to easier tasks, we would face disaster. The crisis began, I think, in February 1921. In the spring of that year we decided unanimously—I did not observe any considerable disagreement among us on this question—to adopt the New Economic Policy. Now, after eighteen months have elapsed, at the close of 1922, we are able to make certain comparisons. What has happened? How have we fared during this period of over eighteen months? What is the result? Has this retreat been of any benefit to us? Has it really saved us, or is the result still indefinite? This is the main question that I put to myself, and I think that this main question is also of first-rate importance to all the Communist Parties; for if the reply is in the negative, we are all doomed. I think that all of us can, with a clear conscience, reply to this question in the affirmative, namely, that the past eighteen months provide positive and absolute proof that we have passed the test. . . .

The salvation of Russia lies not only in a good harvest on the peasant farms—that is not enough; and not only in the good condition of light industry, which provides the peasantry with consumer goods—this, too, is not enough; we also need *heavy* industry. And to put it in a good condition will require several years of work.

Heavy industry needs state subsidies. If we are not able to provide them, we shall be doomed as a civilized state, let alone as a socialist state. In this respect, we have taken a determined step. We have begun to accumulate the funds that we need to put heavy industry on its feet. True, the sum we have obtained so far barely exceeds twenty million gold rubles; but at any rate this sum is available, and it is earmarked exclusively for the purpose of reviving our heavy industry.

I think that, on the whole, I have, as I have promised, briefly outlined the principal elements of our economy, and feel that we may draw the conclusion from all this that the New Economic Policy has already yielded dividends. We already have proof that, as a state, we are able to trade, to maintain our strong positions in agriculture and industry, and to make progress. Practical activity has proved it. I think this is sufficient for us for the time being. We shall have to learn much, and we have realized that we still have much to learn. We have been in power for five years, and during these five years we have been in a state of war. Hence, we have been successful.

This is understandable, because the peasantry were on our side. Probably no one could have supported us more than they did. They were aware that the whiteguards had the landowners behind them, and they hate the landowners more than anything in the world. That is why the peasantry supported us with all their enthusiasm and loyalty. It was not difficult to get the peasantry to defend us against the whiteguards. The peasants, who had always hated war, did all they possibly could in the war against the whiteguards, in the Civil War against the landowners. But this was not all, because in substance it was only a matter of whether power would remain in the hands of the landowners or of the peasants. This was not enough for us. The peasants know that we have seized power for the workers and that our aim is to use this power to establish the socialist system. Therefore, the most important thing for us was to lay the economic foundation for socialist economy. We could not do it directly. We had to do it in a roundabout way. The state capitalism that we have introduced in our country is of a special kind. It does not agree with the usual conception of state capitalism. We hold all the key positions. We hold the land; it belongs to the state. This is very important, although our opponents try to make out that it is of no importance at all. That is untrue. The fact that the land belongs to the state is extremely important, and economically it is also of great practical purport. This we have achieved, and I must say that all our future activities should develop only within that framework. We have already succeeded in making the peasantry content and in reviving both industry and trade. I have already said that our state capitalism differs from state capitalism in the literal sense of the term in that our proletarian state not only owns the land, but also all the vital branches of industry. To begin with, we have leased only a certain number of the small and medium plants, but all the rest remain in our hands. As regards trade, I want to reemphasize that we are trying to found mixed companies, that we are already forming them, i.e., companies in which part of the capital belongs to private capitalists—and foreign capitalists at that—and the other part belongs to the state. Firstly, in this way we are learning how to trade, and that is what we need. Secondly, we are always in a position to dissolve these companies if we deem it necessary, and do not, therefore, run any risks, so to speak. We are learning from the private capitalist and looking round to see how we can progress, and what mistakes we make. It seems to me that I need say no more.

48

Letter to Maxim Gorky
December 6, 1921

The end of compulsory requisitioning, which peasants called "the robber tax," was welcomed in the countryside, but agriculture recovered slowly. The loss of labor, draft animals, and implements in World War I, the Civil War, and the draconian interlude of War Communism was not easily overcome. Disorder, local rebellions, and a severe drought compounded these difficulties. Millions died from starvation in densely populated areas of the Volga, Ukraine, the Urals, and elsewhere in Russia. In July 1921, Herbert Hoover, the U.S. secretary of commerce and president of the American Relief Administration (ARA), offered assistance. Lenin first rejected American aid, but then accepted it with suspicion. The Bolsheviks' international appeal through workers' organizations failed to yield significant results. The ARA organized famine relief in Russia on a wide scale, setting up their own canteens and hiring local staff. Lenin's unwavering suspicion of the ARA and his cynical attitude toward the victims of famine is apparent from the following letter to Maxim Gorky,[24] instructing him to attempt to secure aid from sympathetic British writers. Curiously, Lenin attributes the idea to do this to others rather than to himself.

[24]Maxim Gorky (Aleksey Maksimovich Peshkov, 1868–1936), the Russian writer. In the first years after the October coup d'état, he condemned Bolshevik rule, but he later supported it. From the beginning of the 1920s, he lived abroad.

V. I. Lenin, *Collected Works*, vol. 45 (Moscow: Progress Publishers, 1970), 404.

Dear A[leksey] M[aksimovich]:

I am very sorry to write in haste. I am terribly tired. I've got insomnia. I am going away for treatment.

I have been requested to write to you: would you write to Bernard Shaw[25] asking him to go to America, and to Wells[26] who is said to be in America now, to get them both to help us in collecting aid to the starving?

It would be a good thing if you wrote them.

The starving will then get a bit more.

The famine is very bad.

Make sure to have a good rest and better treatment.[27]

Regards,
Lenin

The Institutionalization of a One-Party System

49

From *We Have Paid Too Much*
April 9, 1922

Lenin was the prime mover in the elimination of all the so-called bourgeois parties after 1917. The Bolsheviks allowed the Mensheviks and Socialist-Revolutionaries to continue to operate for a while, but only under very restricted circumstances. When the Civil War ended, the Bolsheviks unleashed a new wave of terror against the Mensheviks and the

---

[25]George Bernard Shaw (1856–1950), an English writer who spoke in favor of the Bolsheviks and their rule.

[26]H. G. Wells (1866–1946), a British writer with socialist inclinations who visited Russia after the revolution and met with Lenin.

[27]Gorky had long suffered from tuberculosis.

V. I. Lenin, *Collected Works*, vol. 33 (Moscow: Progress Publishers, 1966), 330–33.

SRs. As the political and economic crisis deepened, the Bolsheviks became increasingly intolerant of criticism. During the second half of 1920, Lenin's government began arresting and exiling leading Mensheviks. On December 8, 1921, the Politburo of the Central Committee of the RCP(B), probably under Lenin's direction or supervision, resolved to ban the Mensheviks' political activity, "paying special attention to the eradication of their influence in the industrial centers."[28] *According to the resolution, Mensheviks were to be exiled "administratively to non-proletarian centers"; were banned, along with SRs, from "elective positions connected with personal contact with the broad masses," including trade unions and cooperatives; and were "found guilty" not only of membership in their party (The Russian Social-Democratic Workers' Party), but also of "activities openly or covertly directed against Soviet power."*

The more militant SRs were treated still more harshly. The SR party split in 1921 and then ceased to exist as an independent entity. In February 1922, the Bolsheviks arrested and tried forty-seven of the party's leaders and members. An international outcry ensued among foreign socialists and even some communists. The Bolsheviks sent a high-powered delegation for discussions with representatives of three Internationals (the Second, Two-and-a-Half, and Third) in Berlin (April 1922). The Bolshevik representatives at the meeting bowed to foreign pressure and agreed not to execute the accused SRs. A show trial, the first of many in Soviet history, was held in Moscow in June 1922. The court sentenced fourteen SR prominent leaders to death, but their execution was delayed by the decree of the All-Russian Executive Committee in accord with the unofficial Berlin agreement with the foreign socialists. Lenin was furious that the SR leaders could not be shot and fumed at the Soviet delegation in the following article in Pravda. *Usually, Lenin got his way. Whether the delegates acted on their own without instructions from Lenin or simply ignored his wishes under pressure from western European socialists is unclear.*

Imagine that a Communist has to enter premises in which agents of the bourgeoisie are carrying on their propaganda at a fairly large meeting of workers. Imagine also that the bourgeoisie demands from us a high price for admission to these premises. If the price has not been agreed to beforehand we must bargain, of course, in order not to im-

---

[28] Kuleshov, *Nashe Otechestvo*, vol. 2, 122.

pose too heavy a burden upon our Party funds. If we pay too much for admission to these premises we shall undoubtedly commit an error. But it is better to pay a high price—at all events until we have learned to bargain properly—than to reject an opportunity of speaking to workers who hitherto have been in the exclusive "possession," so to speak, of the reformists, i.e., of the most loyal friends of the bourgeoisie.

This analogy came to my mind when in today's *Pravda* I read a telegram from Berlin stating the terms on which agreement has been reached between the representatives of the three Internationals.

In my opinion our representatives were wrong in agreeing to the following two conditions: first, that the Soviet Government should not apply the death penalty in the case of the forty-seven Socialist-Revolutionaries; second, that the Soviet Government should permit representatives of the three Internationals to be present at the trial.

These two conditions are nothing more or less than a political concession on the part of the revolutionary proletariat to the reactionary bourgeoisie. If anyone has any doubt about the correctness of this definition, then, to reveal the political naiveté of such a person, it is sufficient to ask him the following questions. Would the British or any other contemporary government permit representatives of the three Internationals to attend the trial of Irish workers charged with rebellion? Or the trial of the workers implicated in the recent rebellion in South Africa?[29] Would the British or any other government, in such, or similar circumstances, agree to promise that it would not impose the death penalty on its political opponents? A little reflection over these questions will be sufficient to enable one to understand the following simple truth. All over the world a struggle is going on between the reactionary bourgeoisie and the revolutionary proletariat. In the present case the Communist International, which represents one side in this struggle, makes a political concession to the other side, i.e., the reactionary bourgeoisie; for everybody in the world knows (except those who want to conceal the obvious truth) that the Socialist-Revolutionaries have shot at Communists and have organized revolts against them, and that they have done this actually, and sometimes, officially, in a united front with the whole of the international reactionary bourgeoisie.

The question is—what concession has the international bourgeoisie

---

[29]Lenin had in mind the workers' uprisings in March 1922 in Johannesburg and other cities in South Africa that were due to economic reasons. The uprisings were suppressed, and more than 10,000 people were arrested. Many of the arrested were tried by military tribunals.

made to us in return? There can only be one reply to this question, and it is that no concession has been made to us whatever.

Only arguments which becloud this simple and clear truth of the class struggle, only arguments which throw dust in the eyes of the masses of working people, can obscure this obvious fact. Under the agreement signed in Berlin by the representatives of the Third International we have made two political concessions to the international bourgeoisie. We have obtained no concession in return.

The representatives of the Second and Two-and-a-Half Internationals acted as blackmailers to extort a political concession from the proletariat for the benefit of the bourgeoisie, while emphatically refusing, or at any rate making no attempt, to induce the international bourgeoisie to make some political concession to the revolutionary proletariat. Of course, this incontrovertible political fact was obscured by shrewd bourgeois diplomats (the bourgeoisie has been training members of its class to become good diplomats for many centuries); but the attempt to obscure the fact does not change it in the least. Whether the various representatives of the Second and Two-and-a-Half Internationals are in direct or indirect collusion with the bourgeoisie is a matter of tenth-rate importance in the present case. We do not accuse them of being in direct collusion. The question of whether there has been direct collusion or fairly intricate, indirect connection has nothing to do with the case. The only point that has anything to do with it is that as a result of the pressure of the representatives of the Second and Two-and-a-Half Internationals, the Communist International has made a political concession to the international bourgeoisie and has obtained no concession in return.

What conclusion should be drawn from this?

First, that Comrades Radek,[30] Bukharin and the others who represented the Communist International acted wrongly. . . .

The mistake that Comrades Radek, Bukharin and the others made is not a grave one, especially as our only risk is that the enemies of Soviet Russia may be encouraged by the result of Berlin Conference to make two or three perhaps successful attempts on the lives of certain persons; for they know beforehand that they can shoot at Communists in the expectation that conferences like the Berlin Conference will hinder the Communists from shooting at them.

---

[30]Karl Berngardovich Radek (1885–1939), a Polish and German Social Democrat, then a Russian Communist. In 1920–1924, he was a member of the Executive Committee of the Communist International.

50

Letter to I. V. Stalin

July 17, 1922

After eliminating all organized political opposition, Lenin sought to eradicate the remaining intellectual opposition. In the summer of 1922, he moved to expel a large group of intellectuals and artists with diverse political views. This group from the cultural and scientific elite of Russia included doctors, scientists, philosophers, political activists, and writers. Lenin's preoccupation with suppressing intellectual opponents and his concern that this operation be carried out fully is apparent from the following letter to Stalin, as is Lenin's belief that even the few surviving private publishers were a danger. Note his distinction between those that he feels can be safely exiled and others, such as the journalist I. G. Lezhnev, whom he prefers to keep in Bolshevik hands. Two months later, Lenin sent the VChK [Cheka] a list of 120 well-known politicians, scientists, professors, and other real and potential intellectual "enemies," asking who had been exiled, who was in prison, and who had been freed and why.[31]

Comrade Stalin!

On the matter of deporting the Mensheviks, Popular Socialists,[32] Kadets, and the like from Russia, I would like to ask several questions in view of the fact that this operation, initiated before my leave, has not been completed to this day.

---

[31]V. I. Lenin, *Neizvestnye dokumenty* 1891–1922 (Moscow: ROSSPEN, 1999), 550–57.

[32]Popular Socialists (*Narodnyie Sotsialisty*)—members of the Working People's Socialist Party (*Trodovaia Narodno-Sotsialisticheskaia Partiia*). The party stayed on the right wing of the socialist camp. It was banished in 1918.

Richard Pipes, ed., *The Unknown Lenin: From the Secret Archive* (New Haven, Conn., and London: Yale University Press, 1996), 168–69.

Resolutely to "uproot" all Popular Socialists? Peshekhonov,[33] Mia-kotin,[34] Gornfeld?[35] Petrishchev,[36] and the others. I think all of them should be deported. They are more harmful than any SR, because more cunning. Also A. N. Potresov,[37] Izgoev,[38] and **the entire** staff of Economist[39] (**Ozerov**[40] and **many, many others**). Mensheviks: Rozanov[41] (a physician, cunning), Vigdorchik[42] (Migulo[43] or some name like that), Lyubov Nikolaevna Radchenko[44] and her young daughter (said to be malicious enemies of Bolshevism); N. A. Rozkkov[45] (he must be deported; he is incorrigible); S. A. [L.] Frank[46] (author of *Metodologiia*). A commission under the supervision of Mantsev,[47] Messing,[48] and others should submit a list of several **hundred** such gentlemen, who

[33]A. V. Peshekhonov (1867–1933), one of the leaders of the People's Socialist Party. In 1922, he was exiled from Russia.
[34]V. A. Miakotin (1867–1937), one of the leaders of the Working People's Socialist Party and a historian. In 1922, he was exiled from Russia.
[35]A. G. Gornfeld (1867–1941), a journalist, a collaborator, and the author of many Russian magazines. Exiled from Russia in 1922.
[36]A. B. Petrishchev (1872– ?), a writer and member of the Working People's Socialist Party. Exiled from Russia in 1922.
[37]A. N. Potresov (1869–1934), one of the founders of the Russian social democracy. After the Bolsheviks seized power, he was repressed and exiled abroad in 1922.
[38]A. Izgoev (1872–1935), a journalist and member of the Cadet Party. In 1922, he was exiled abroad.
[39]*Economist*—the magazine of the Russian Technical Society. The magazine was published for a short period of time in Petrograd in 1921–1922 and then closed by the authorities.
[40]I. Kh. Ozerov (1869–1942), an economist and professor at Moscow and St. Petersburg Universities. After 1917, he worked in the People's Commissariat of Finance of the RSFSR.
[41]V. N. Rozanov (1876–1939), a medical doctor and Menshevik. In August 1919, he was arrested, and after the amnesty of 1921, he did not participate in politics.
[42]N. A. Vigdorchik (1874–1954), a medical doctor and Menshevik. He did not take part in political activities after 1906.
[43]Migulo (Makula), a medical doctor and Menshevik.
[44]L. N. Radchenko (1871–1962), a medical doctor and Menshevik. From 1918, he did not participate in politics. He also worked as a statistician.
[45]N. A. Rozkkov (1868–1927), a historian. From 1905–1910, he was a Bolshevik, then a Menshevik. In 1922, he was exiled to the city of Pskov, where he continued his research.
[46]S. L. Frank (1877–1950), a religious philosopher and professor. In 1922, he was exiled from Russia. Lenin had in mind Frank's book *Ocherk metodologii obshchestvennyh nauk* (Survey of the Methodology of Social Sciences).
[47]V. N. Mantsev (1889–1939). In 1921–1923, he was the chairman of the Ukrainian Extraordinary Commission and the people's commissar for internal affairs of Ukraine.
[48]S. A. Messing (1890–1937?), from 1920, one of the chiefs of the All-Russian Extraordinary Commission.

must be deported abroad without mercy. We will purge Russia for a long time to come.

Regarding Lezhnev[49] (formerly of *Den'*), we should reflect a great deal about whether he should not be deported. He will always be extremely crafty, as far as I can judge from the articles of his that I have read.

Ozerov, like **the entire** staff of *Economist*, are the most ruthless enemies. The lot—out of Russia.

This must be done at once. Before the end of the trial of the SRs— no later. Arrest several hundred and **without stating** the reasons— out with you, gentlemen!

All the authors from *Dom literatorov* [House of writers][50] and the Petrograd *Mysl'*;[51] Kharkov should be ransacked—**we don't know it**, it is a "foreign country" for us. We must purge **quickly, no later** than by the end of the SRs' trial.

Note the literary figures in Petrograd (addresses in *Novaia Russkaia Kniga*, no. 4, 1922, p. 37) and the list of private publishers (p. 29).

> With communist greetings,
> *Lenin*

Toward a Single Spiritual and Cultural System

Lenin wanted to remake Russia under Bolshevik rule. He expected culture, like the state, to express the values and interests of the proletariat. He thought the ruling class in bourgeois countries used the printed word to maintain their hegemony and felt the Bolsheviks should do likewise. On seizing power, he and his colleagues nationalized leading newspapers, seized control of the mass print media, and set out to create a public culture supportive of their great project. On

---

[49]I. G. Lezhnev (1890–1955), a journalist. In the beginning of 1922, he edited the Moscow magazine *Novaia Rossiia* (The New Russia), which was closed by the authorities. After that he was exiled abroad, but returned to Russia in 1930. Before the Russian Revolution, he edited the liberal magazine *Den'* (The Day) in St. Petersburg from 1912 through 1917. This magazine was also closed by the Bolsheviks.

[50]Lenin had in mind The House of Men of Letters in Petrograd, which in 1921–1922 edited the magazine *Letopis'* (Annals).

[51]*Mysl'* (Thought), the magazine of St. Petersburg's Philosophical Society, was closed by the authorities in 1922.

November 9, 1917, under Lenin's signature, the Bolsheviks published the "Decree on the Press," closing all newspapers that showed "open opposition or insubordination to the worker-peasant government."[52] In his most utopian essay, *State and Revolution* (1916), Lenin had expressed a more open view of proletarian rule (Document 5). Yet with the machinery of state in his hands, he denied his opponents a platform. "To tolerate these [bourgeois] newspapers means not to be a socialist," he warned a leftist critic.[53] In 1918, the Bolsheviks closed the remaining socialist newspapers and solidified their monopoly of the printed word.

Lenin considered literature and the arts weapons in the revolutionary armory. He hesitated to dictate a single style for socialist culture, but he intervened whenever he saw something he disliked. He permitted what he considered harmless bourgeois culture to survive so long as he did not find it too expensive, too critical, or too independent. When the market in cultural goods vanished, all arts became public arts and all artists became de facto state employees. Faced with opposition from the intelligentsia, the Bolsheviks accepted the support of some avant-garde artists and writers, and Lenin initially tolerated them, perhaps because of the prestige they lent Bolshevik rule.

51

Letter to A. V. Lunacharsky
May 6, 1921

Vladimir Mayakovsky was probably the revolution's greatest poet. He claimed to have been a Bolshevik from age thirteen, and some party leaders delighted in his revolutionary enthusiasm. Lenin mistrusted him, however, for his ties to the Futurists, a group notable for an eagerness to shock.[54]

[52]*TsK KPSS O partiinoi i sovetskoi pechati. Sbornik dokumentov* (Moscow: Pravda, 1954), 173.
[53]V. I. Lenin and M. D. Orakhelashvili, *Dekrety Oktiabr'skoi revoliutsii: pravitel'- stvennye akty, podpisannye ili utverzhdennye Leninym, kak predsedatelem Sovnarkoma* (Moscow: Partiinoe izd-vo, 1933).
[54]Futurism was a literary movement that began in Italy before World War I and immediately spread to Russia. Russian futurists, including Mayakovsky, supported the Bolshevik Revolution but Lenin, whose cultural tastes were conservative, abhorred their experiments with language.

V. I. Lenin, *Collected Works*, vol. 45 (Moscow: Progress Publishers, 1970), 138–39.

In the following document, Lenin jokingly suggests that Minister of Culture Anatoly Lunacharsky[55] should be flogged for publishing Mayakovsky's poem "150,000,000." In this poem, Mayakovsky optimistically hails 150,000,000 Ivans (the Soviet population in 1919) as a new creative force.

Aren't you ashamed to vote for printing 5,000 copies of Mayakovsky's[56] "150,000,000"?

It is nonsense, stupidity, double-dyed stupidity and affectation.

I believe such things should be published one in ten, and *not more than 1,500 copies*, for libraries and cranks.

As for Lunacharsky, he should be flogged for his futurism.

Lenin

52

Letter to V. M. Molotov for the Politburo of the CC of RCP(B)

January 12, 1922

Lenin expresses his eagerness to conserve economic resources for other tasks more vital to the revolution in a letter to V. M. Molotov, a candidate member of the Politburo and future ally of Stalin. In the letter, he demands the closure of the Bolshoi Theater, once the glory of Russian performing arts, because it is too costly to run and maintain. Note his reference to "stricter measures," particularly better control over the Central Committee, which had many more members than the Politburo.

[55]Anatolii Vasilievich Lunacharsky (1875–1933). In 1917–1929, he was the people's commissar of education in the Soviet government.

[56]Vladimir Vladimirovich Mayakovsky (1893–1930), a Russian poet. Before 1917 and in the first years of Bolshevik power, he was a futurist, then a leading Soviet writer.

V. I. Lenin, *Collected Works*, vol. 45 (Moscow: Progress Publishers, 1970), 428–29.

Comrade Molotov,

Having learned from Kamenev that the C.P.C.[57] has unanimously adopted Lunacharsky's absolutely improper proposal to preserve the Bolshoi Opera and Ballet, I suggest that the Politburo should resolve:

1. To instruct the Presidium of the All-Russian C.E.C.[58] to rescind the C.P.C. decision.

2. Of the opera and ballet company, to leave only a few dozen actors for Moscow and Petrograd so that their performance (both operatic and choreographic) should pay,[59] i.e., by eliminating all large expenses on properties, etc.

3. Of the thousands of millions saved in this way at least one-half to be allotted to wiping out illiteracy and for reading rooms.

4. To summon Lunacharsky for five minutes, to hear the last word of the accused, it being pointed out to him and to all People's Commissars that in future introducing and putting to the vote of resolutions like the one now being rescinded by the C.C., will entail stricter measures on the part of the C.C.

Lenin

53

From *The Tasks of the Youth Leagues*
October 2, 1920

The Komsomol (Young Communist League), the youth arm of the Communist Party, was important in the countryside, where regular party members were scarce. In the following speech to the delegates at the Komsomol's Third Congress, Lenin stressed the importance of education,

---

[57]Counsel of People Commissars (CPC), the government of Soviet Russia.

[58]Central Executive Committee (CEC), the legislative body, which worked between All-Russian Congresses of Soviets.

[59]For instance, through participation by opera singers and ballet dancers in all kinds of concerts, etc. [Lenin's note.]

V. I. Lenin, *Collected Works*, vol. 31 (Moscow: Progress Publishers, 1965), 290–93.

the correct training of future leaders, and inculcating "Communist ethics." What does Lenin mean by "Communist ethics"? What value judgments does he urge the young communists to adopt, and how does he instruct them to deal with the problem of peasants unwilling to give up their surplus grain voluntarily?

I first of all shall deal here with the question of communist ethics.

You must train yourselves to be Communists. It is the task of the Youth League to organize its practical activities in such a way that, by learning, organizing, uniting and fighting, its members shall train both themselves and all those who look to it for leadership; it should train Communists. The entire purpose of training, educating and teaching the youth of today should be to imbue them with communist ethics.

But is there such a thing as communist ethics? Is there such a thing as communist morality? Of course, there is. It is often suggested that we have no ethics of our own; very often the bourgeoisie accuse us Communists of rejecting all morality. This is a method of confusing the issue, of throwing dust in the eyes of the workers and peasants.

In what sense do we reject ethics, reject morality?

In the sense given to it by the bourgeoisie, who based ethics on God's commandments. On this point we, of course, say that we do not believe in God, and that we know perfectly well that the clergy, the landowners and the bourgeoisie invoked the name of God so as to further their own interests as exploiters. Or, instead of basing ethics on the commandments of morality, on the commandments of God, they based it on idealist or semi-idealist phrases, which always amounted to something very similar to God's commandments. . . .

The class struggle is continuing; it has merely changed its forms. It is the class struggle of the proletariat to prevent the return of the old exploiters, to unite in a single union the scattered masses of unenlightened peasants. The class struggle is continuing and it is our task to subordinate all interests to that struggle. Our communist morality is also subordinated to that task. We say: morality is what serves to destroy the old exploiting society and to unite all the working people around the proletariat, which is building up a new, a communist society.

Communist morality is that which serves this struggle and unites the working people against all exploitation, against all petty private property; for petty property puts into the hands of one person that which has been created by the labor of the whole of society.

54

From *Letter to V. M. Molotov*
for the Members of the CC of RCP(B)
March 19, 1922

Lenin agreed with Marx's statement in the introduction to his book A
Contribution to the Critique or Hegel's Philosophy of Right *(1844)
that religion was "the opium of the people." He decried it as an obstacle
to socialism and blamed it for the peasants' passivity and other social
ills. Russia was home to many religions, but Russian Orthodox Christianity was the chief source of spiritual opposition to Bolshevism even
though the church as a state institution under the tsar had lacked the
independence of Western Christian denominations. Since the church was
also an obstacle to the cultural system Lenin and his followers sought to
promote, they divested it of its power, landed property, educational institutions, and other assets. They also banned religious marriage and
replaced it with a civil procedure. Finally, on January 23, 1918 (February 5), the government decreed the separation of church and state and
deprived the institution of its official status, eventually preventing
churches from levying dues and clergy from voting for or serving in soviets. While the Bolsheviks desecrated relics and campaigned against religion, the Russian Orthodox Patriarch and high clergy incited the people
against the revolutionaries, and some bishops even joined anti-Bolshevik
forces in the Civil War.*

*Lenin and his colleagues used the famine of 1921–1922 as a pretext
to undermine the church. On February 23, 1922, the government
published a decree ordering the seizure of Orthodox treasures for sale
abroad, including bejeweled icons, crosses, and other precious religious
articles. The church resisted, and a bloody clash between Bolshevik militants and church activists ensued in the small town of Shuya. Lenin
explained his plans to use the events in Shuya in a letter to Molotov, an
excerpt of which follows. The letter is marked "strictly secret" and was
excluded from Soviet editions of his works. In fact, Lenin repeats the
word "secret" several times in this document. Note that Lenin orders
Kalinin, formally the head of state and ostensibly the leader friendliest to*

Richard Pipes, ed., *The Unknown Lenin: From the Secret Archive* (New Haven, Conn.,
and London: Yale University Press, 1996), 152–55.

the peasantry, to assume public responsibility for the campaign, and he excludes Trotsky, who had much greater power as head of the Red Army, from a public role because Trotsky was Jewish, which would have complicated the struggle. Lenin never concealed his hostility to the Orthodox Church. Readers of the following document may consider his strategy for undermining it in this instance.

Top Secret
Do not make copies for any reason,
but have each Politburo member (as
well as Comrade Kalinin) write his
comments on this document.
Lenin[60]

To Comrade Molotov for the Politburo members

Regarding the event in Shuia which is already on the agenda for discussion by the Politburo, I think a firm decision must be made immediately regarding a general plan of struggle in the given direction. . . .

I think that here our enemy is committing an enormous strategic mistake in trying to drag us into a decisive battle at a time when it is particularly hopeless and particularly disadvantageous for him. On the contrary, for us this moment is not only exceptionally favorable but generally the only moment when we can, with ninety-nine out of a hundred chances of total success, smash the enemy and secure for ourselves an indispensable position for many decades to come. It is precisely now and only now, when in the starving regions people are eating human flesh, and hundreds if not thousands of corpses are littering the roads, that we can (and therefore must) carry out the confiscation of church valuables with the most savage and merciless energy, not stopping [short of] crushing any resistance. It is precisely now and only now that the enormous majority of the peasant mass will be for us or at any rate will not be in a condition to support in any decisive way that handful of Black Hundred clergy[61] and reactionary

---

[60]Molotov noted on the document: "Agreed. However, [I] propose not to spread the campaign to all provinces [in the text, gubernias], but only to those where there are substantial valuables, concentrating the forces and attention of the Party there."

[61]This refers to prerevolutionary right-wing gangs known as the "black hundred," who attacked Jews and others.

urban petty bourgeoisie who can and want to attempt a policy of violent resistance to the Soviet decree.

We must, come what may, carry out the confiscation of church valuables in the most decisive and rapid manner, so as to secure for ourselves a fund of several hundred million gold rubles (one must recall the gigantic wealth of some of the monasteries and abbeys). Without this fund, no government work in general, no economic construction in particular, and no defense of our position in Genoa[62] especially is even conceivable. No matter what happens, we must lay our hands on a fund of several hundred million gold rubles (and perhaps even several billion). And this can be done successfully only now. All considerations indicate that later we will be unable to do this, because no other moment except that of desperate hunger will give us a mood among the broad peasant masses that will guarantee us the sympathy of these masses or at least their neutrality, in the sense that victory in the struggle for the confiscation of the valuables will be indisputable and entirely ours. . . .

Only Comrade Kalinin should publicly undertake measures of any kind—Comrade Trotsky should at no time and under no circumstances speak out [on this matter] in the press or before the public in any other manner. . . .

At the party congress arrange a secret meeting on this matter of all or nearly all the delegates, together with the chief functionaries of the GPU, the People's Commissariat of Justice, and the Revolutionary Tribunal.[63] At this meeting, pass a secret resolution of the congress that the confiscation of valuables, in particular of the richest abbeys, monasteries, and churches, should be conducted with merciless determination, unconditionally stopping at nothing, and in the briefest possible time. The greater the number of representatives of the reactionary clergy and reactionary bourgeoisie we succeed in executing for this reason, the better. We must teach these people a lesson right now, so that they will not dare even to think of any resistance for several decades.

In order to oversee the most rapid and successful implementation of these measures, appoint a special commission right at the [Eleventh Party] congress, i.e., at its secret meeting, with the mandatory partici-

---

[62]See page 24 of the introduction for a fuller discussion of Russia's negotiations with Germany in Genoa, which resulted in the Treaty of Rapallo.

[63]Lenin had in mind the Eleventh Congress of the RCP(B). The point he proposed was not put on its agenda. In the documentary materials, there is no mention of a meeting about churches during the congress.

pation of Comrade Trotsky and Comrade Kalinin, without any publicity about this commission, so that the subordination of all operations to it is secured and conducted not in the name of the commission but through the customary Soviet and party procedures. Appoint the best—especially responsible—[party] workers for this measure in the richest abbeys, monasteries, and churches.

Lenin

19 March '22

I request Comrade Molotov to try to circulate this letter to members of the Politburo today (without making copies) and ask them to return it to the secretary immediately upon reading, with a brief notation about whether each Politburo member is in accord with the principle or if the letter raises any disagreements.

Lenin

19 March '22
Dictation taken over the telephone.
M. Volodicheva[64]

---

[64] Mariia Akimovna Volodicheva (1881–1973), an assistant secretary in the Council of Labor and Defense.

4

The Sick Leader:
De Facto Removal from Power

Lenin's health began to fail in 1921. In August 1921, he wrote to M. Gorky, "I am so tired that I am incapable of the slightest work."[1] Undoubtedly, the political and personal failures of the past year (the defeat in Poland, the failure of War Communism, and the death of his former lover Inessa Armand[2]), as well as Lenin's efforts to solve the regime's economic, political, cultural, and other problems single-handedly, contributed to his health crisis.

On May 25, 1922, Lenin had his first stroke, which paralyzed his right arm and right leg. He initially lost the ability to speak. But his condition gradually improved, and he participated in several congresses and meetings in October–November 1922, although his control over his mental processes was uneven. Sometimes he did not fully understand what he was reading when he read aloud from a prepared text. The old Bolshevik and Politburo member L. B. Kamenev told Lenin's doctors that Lenin had once read the same page of a speech twice without realizing it.[3]

Lenin suffered another significant stroke in mid-December 1922. It was not as serious as the first, however, and he soon tried to work again. Nevertheless, his colleagues, led by Stalin and others including Zinoviev and Kamenev, as well as local leaders, decided to remove him from power and concentrate power in their own hands as quickly as possible.

Stalin had been appointed general secretary of the party in the

---

[1] M. Gorky, *Days with Lenin* (London: International Publishers, 1932), 52.

[2] Although the Bolsheviks were officially and publicly puritanical, many of them had lovers, and this was tolerated in the inner circle, especially when the lovers were communists, too. Inessa Armand (1874–1920) was the daughter of a French actor who married a Russian. Armand met Lenin in 1910 and became his follower and then his mistress. After 1917, she worked for the Communist International. She died of cholera.

[3] Beryl Williams, *Lenin* (London: Longman, 2000), 190.

spring of 1922. His position at first seemed organizational rather than political. Yet Stalin was also a member of the Politburo, and this dual position gave him great authority. During the first months of his secretariat, he began to gain control over the local bureaucracies of republics, regions, and great cities. Although he shared power with Kamenev and Zinoviev, he held the chief position. After Lenin's serious second stroke, Stalin arranged the decision of the Central Committee on December 18, 1922, "to make comrade Stalin personally responsible for the isolation of Vladimir Il'ich with regard to both his personal relations with officials and his correspondence."[4]

55

Letter to Stalin for Politburo of RCP(B) CC

June 15, 1922

After Lenin's first stroke, Stalin tried to isolate him. When Lenin refused treatment by German doctors, Stalin overruled him on political grounds. In the middle of June 1922, Lenin and Stalin exchanged letters, beginning with one in which Lenin begged his one-time protégé to free him from the German doctors. Perhaps the Germans irritated Lenin by recognizing his powerlessness, or perhaps he was simply suspicious of their intentions.

June 15, 1922

To Stalin for the Politburo

I beg you most humbly to liberate me from Klemperer.[5] [His] extreme concern and caution can drive a person out of his mind and cause trouble.

---

[4] *Izvestiia TsRK KPSS* (1989, 12), 191.
[5] G. Klemperer was a German doctor and professor who, along with Professor O. Ferster, treated Lenin after his first stroke.

Richard Pipes, ed., *The Unknown Lenin: From the Secret Archive* (New Haven, Conn., and London: Yale University Press, 1996), 165.

If there is no other way, I agree to send him on a scientific assignment.

I strongly urge you to rid me of Foerster. I am more than extremely satisfied with my doctors Kramer and Kozhevnikov. Russian cannot stand German meticulousness, and Foerster and Klemperer have already participated enough in the consultation.

15 June

Lenin

I certify the authenticity. M. Ulianova[6]

56

From *Letter to the Congress: Continuation of the Notes*
December 24, 1922

Once Stalin had gained the Central Committee's approval to control Lenin's access to family, friends, and party officials, he quickly put the former leader under de facto house arrest. At an unofficial meeting on December 24, Stalin, Bukharin, and Kamenev agreed to keep Lenin completely isolated from political activities. They agreed to "allow" Lenin to dictate "notes," but only for the record and not for circulation. Lenin struck back at Stalin and other leaders in his "Letter to the Congress," known as his "political testament." All members of the Thirteenth Party Congress in 1924 heard the letter read to them in separate groups. The Congress then agreed to suppress the letter, and under Stalin mention of it often led to arrest or even execution. It first appeared publicly in a shortened version designed to soften its impact soon after Stalin's death in the 1950s and was published in the fifth edition of Lenin's collected works. The Russian historian Yuri Buranov restored the original. The

[6]M. I. Ulianova (1878–1937) was Lenin's younger sister.

Yuri Buranov, *Lenin's Will: Falsified and Forbidden. From the Secret Archives of the Former Soviet Union* (Amherst, N.Y.: Prometheus Books, 1994), 214–16.

following text and notes from December 1922 and early January 1923 are from Buranov's book, which was not published in Russia until the 1990s. Trotsky passed Lenin's "Letter to the Congress" to his American follower Max Eastman, but before Eastman could publish it, Trotsky submitted to party discipline and denied its existence. Eastman published the complete text anyway in the New York Times *on October 18, 1926. In the letter, Lenin proposed avoiding a party split by increasing the size of the Central Committee. He also suggested expanding the chief administrative bodies of the party, perhaps with an eye to returning to power. Curiously, and possibly with his own return to governing in mind, Lenin denigrated almost all the well-known leaders of the party and state. He even attacked Iurii L. Pyatakov, who had no apparent interest in succeeding him and was only a candidate member of the Central Committee. Such proposals reveal how little Lenin understood the severity of his illness and the intentions of his opponents.*

By stability of the Central Committee, of which I spoke above, I mean measures against a split, as far as such measures can at all be taken. . . .

Our Party relies on two classes and therefore its instability would be possible and its downfall inevitable if there were no agreement between those two classes. In that event this or that measure, and generally all talk about the stability of our CC, would be futile. No measures of any kind could prevent a split in such a case. But I hope that this is too remote a future and too improbable an event to talk about.

I have in mind stability as a guarantee against a split in the immediate future, and I intend to deal here with a few ideas concerning personal qualities.

I think that from this standpoint the prime factors in the question of stability are such members of the CC as Stalin and Trotsky. I think relations between them make up the greater part of the danger of a split, which could be avoided; and this purpose, in my opinion, would be served, among other things, by increasing the number of CC members to 50 or 100.

Comrade Stalin, having become General Secretary, has unlimited authority concentrated in his hands, and I am not sure whether he will always be capable of using that authority with sufficient caution. Comrade Trotsky, on the other hand, as his struggle against the CC on the question of the People's Commissariat for Communications[7] has already proved, is distinguished not only by outstanding ability. He is personally perhaps the most capable man in the present CC, but he has displayed excessive self-assurance and shown excessive preoccupation with the purely administrative side of the work.

These two qualities of the two outstanding leaders of the present CC can inadvertently lead to a split, and if our Party does not take steps to avert this, the split may come unexpectedly.

I shall not give any further appraisals of the personal qualities of other members of the CC. I shall just recall that the October episode with Zinoviev and Kamenev was, of course, no accident,[8] but neither can the blame for it be laid upon them personally, any more than non-Bolshevism can upon Trotsky.[9]

Speaking of the young CC members, I wish to say a few words about Bukharin and Pyatakov.[10] They are, in my opinion, the most outstanding figures (among the youngest ones), and the following must be borne in mind about them: Bukharin is not only a most valuable and major theorist of the Party; he is also rightly considered the favorite of the whole Party, but his theoretical views can be classified as fully Marxist only with great reserve, for there is something scholastic about him (he has never made a study of dialectics, and, I think, never fully understood it).

December 25. As for Pyatakov, he is unquestionably a man of outstanding will and outstanding ability, but shows too much zeal for administrating and the administrative side of the work to be relied upon in a serious political matter.

Both of these remarks, of course, are made only for the present, on the assumption that both these outstanding and devoted Party work-

---

[7]Lenin had in mind several declarations by Trotsky in 1920 in which the latter planned to place railroads and other communications under the Red Army—to militarize them.

[8]"October episode" refers to the fact that Kamenev and Zinoviev opposed the Bolshevik seizure of power by force in the October Revolution.

[9]Until the summer of 1917, Trotsky staked out a centrist position between Bolsheviks and Mensheviks. He joined the Bolsheviks only after returning to Russia in May 1917. At the Sixth Congress of the Bolsheviks (July–August 1917), he became a member of the party and was elected to the CC.

[10]G. L. Pyatakov (1890–1937) was the chairman of the central board of the coal industry in the Donets Basin from 1920.

ers fail to find an occasion to enhance their knowledge and amend their one-sidedness.

Lenin

December 25, 1922
Taken down by M. V.

Addition to the Letter of December 24, 1922

Stalin is too rude, and this defect, although quite tolerable in our midst and in dealings among us Communists, becomes intolerable in a General Secretary. That is why I suggest that the comrades think about a way of removing Stalin from that post and appointing another man in his stead who in all other respects differs from Comrade Stalin in having only one advantage, namely, that of being more tolerant, more loyal, more polite and more considerate to the comrades, less capricious, etc. This circumstance may appear to be a negligible detail. But I think that from the standpoint of what I wrote above about the relationship between Stalin and Trotsky it is not a detail, or it is a detail that can assume decisive importance.

Lenin

Taken down by L. F.

57

Letter to I. V. Stalin
March 5, 1923

A final conflict between Lenin and Stalin arose after Stalin was rude to Lenin's wife, Krupskaia. After she complained, Lenin sent Stalin the following hostile letter. Almost immediately after sending this letter, Lenin suffered another damaging stroke that effectively ended his conscious life. The fact that Lenin did not send Trotsky, until now a trusted lieutenant,

V. I. Lenin, *Collected Works*, vol. 45 (Moscow: Progress Publishers, 1970), 607–8.

a copy of this letter raises questions about Lenin's loyalties and last thoughts. Although they had disagreed about many issues in the past, Trotsky had become Lenin's loyal follower. Perhaps Lenin's decision to keep this letter from Trotsky reveals a lasting mistrust.

Top secret
Personal

Copy to Comrades Kamenev and Zinoviev

Dear Comrade Stalin:

You have been so rude to summon my wife to the telephone and use bad language. Although she had told you that she was prepared to forget this, the fact nevertheless became known through her to Zinoviev and Kamenev. I have no intention of forgetting so easily what has been done against me, and it goes without saying that what has been done against my wife I consider having been done against me as well. I ask you, therefore, to think it over whether you are prepared to withdraw what you have said and to make your apologies, or whether you prefer that relations between us should be broken off.

Respectfully yours,
Lenin

Lenin's Last Thoughts

Did Lenin, during his last months, begin reconsidering the policies he had set in place? Did he have second thoughts about employing terror and compulsion to build socialism? From late December 1922 until his incapacitating stroke on March 6 or 7, 1923, Lenin wrote commentaries and proposals on government policy despite his isolation by Stalin and Stalin's supporters. Yet Lenin's last articles lack his usual coherent argumentation and summations, suggesting that his illness may have affected his acuity.

58

From *On Co-operation*
January 4 and 6, 1923

Some documents from Lenin's last months show inconsistencies and inattention to reality, such as the following note on co-operatives, which Lenin and other Bolshevik leaders had previously condemned as bourgeois. Did Lenin realize how impractical his "co-operative plan" was given the realities of Soviet political life? He probably did not. The Bolsheviks had restricted co-operatives at the outset, as they did all non-party organizations. Is he suggesting in the following document that the co-operatives should function as independent organizations with leaders not subject to party control?

It seems to me that not enough attention is being paid to the co-operative movement in our country. Not everyone understands that now, since the time of the October Revolution and quite apart from NEP (on the contrary, in this connection we must say—because of NEP), our co-operative movement has become one of great significance. . . .

Indeed, since political power is in the hands of the working class, since this political power owns all the means of production, the only task, indeed, that remains for us is to organize the population in co-operative societies. With most of the population organized in co-operatives, the socialism which in the past was legitimately treated with ridicule, scorn and contempt by those who were rightly convinced that it was necessary to wage the class struggle, the struggle for political power, etc., will achieve its aim automatically. But not all comrades realize how vastly, how infinitely important it is now to organize the population of Russia in co-operative societies. By adopting NEP we made a concession to the peasant as a trader, to the principle of private trade; it is precisely for this reason (contrary to what some people think) that the co-operative movement is of such immense importance. All we actually need under NEP is to organize the

V. I. Lenin, *Collected Works*, vol. 33 (Moscow: Progress Publishers, 1965), 467–71.

population of Russia in co-operative societies on a sufficiently large scale, for we have now found that degree of combination of private interest, of private commercial interest, with state supervision and control of this interest, that degree of its subordination to the common interests which was formerly the stumbling-block for very many socialists. Indeed, the power of the state over all large-scale means of production, political power in the hands of the proletariat, the alliance of this proletariat with the many millions of small and very small peasants, the assured proletarian leadership of the peasantry, etc. — is this not all that is necessary to build a complete socialist society out of co-operatives, out of co-operatives alone, which we formerly ridiculed as huckstering and which from a certain aspect we have the right to treat as such now, under NEP? Is this not all that is necessary to build a complete socialist society? It is still not the building of socialist society, but it is all that is necessary and sufficient for it.

It is this very circumstance that is underestimated by many of our practical workers. They look down upon our co-operative societies, failing to appreciate their exceptional importance, first, from the standpoint of principle (the means of production are owned by the state), and, second, from the standpoint of transition to the new system by means that are the *simplest, easiest and most acceptable to the peasant.*

But this again is of fundamental importance. It is one thing to draw up fantastic plans for building socialism through all sorts of workers' associations, and quite another to learn to build socialism in practice in such a way that *every* small peasant could take part in it. That is the very stage we have now reached. And there is no doubt that, having reached it, we are taking too little advantage of it.

We went too far when we introduced NEP, but not because we attached too much importance to the principle of free enterprise and trade — we went too far because we lost sight of the co-operatives, because we now underrate the co-operatives, because we are already beginning to forget the vast importance of the co-operatives from the above two points of view. . . .

Co-operation must be politically so organized that it will not only generally and always enjoy certain privileges, but that these privileges should be of a purely material nature (a favorable bank-rate, etc.). The co-operatives must be granted state loans that are greater, if only by a little, than the loans we grant to private enterprises, even to heavy industry, etc. . . .

In conclusion: a number of economic, financial and banking privileges must be granted to the co-operatives—this is the way our socialist state must promote the new principle on which the population must be organized. But this is only the general outline of the task; it does not define and depict in detail the entire content of the practical task, i.e., we must find what form of "bonus" to give for joining the co-operatives (and the terms on which we should give it), the form of bonus by which we shall assist the co-operatives sufficiently, the form of bonus that will produce the civilized co-operator. And given social ownership of the means of production, given the class victory of the proletariat over the bourgeoisie, the system of civilized co-operators is the system of socialism.

59

From *The Question of Nationalities or "Autonomization"*

December 30, 1922

In his final months, Lenin challenged Stalin on several issues. In the following document, Lenin criticizes Stalin's plans for a unified Soviet state, despite the fact that the Soviet Union was already, for all intents and purposes, such a state at the end of 1922. While Russia, Ukraine, Byelorussia, and Trans-Caucasia were formally independent, they were in reality governed by the party apparatus, like the rest of the country. In 1922, Stalin proposed their autonomization, *that is, their formal inclusion into Russia with a promise of some self-rule and, therefore, the end of their presumed independence as republics. Stalin agreed to Lenin's modifications of his proposals because they were unlikely to change the centralized dictatorship under communist leadership and because his own power was still limited.*

Lenin began dictating the following notes on the issue the very day the Union of the Soviet Republics (USSR) was proclaimed.

V. I. Lenin, *Collected Works*, vol. 36 (Moscow: Progress Publishers, 1966), 605–7.

I suppose I have been very remiss with respect to the workers of Russia for not having intervened energetically and decisively enough in the notorious question of autonomization, which, it appears, is officially called the question of the union of Soviet socialist republics.

When this question arose last summer, I was ill; and then in autumn I relied too much on my recovery and on the October and December plenary meetings giving me an opportunity of intervening in this question. However, I did not manage to attend the October Plenary Meeting (when this question came up) or the one in December, and so the question passed me by almost completely. . . .

It is said that a united apparatus was needed. Where did that assurance come from? Did it now come from that same Russian apparatus which, as I pointed out in one of the preceding sections of my diary, we took over from tsarism and slightly anointed with Soviet oil?

There is no doubt that that measure should have been delayed somewhat until we could say that we vouched for our apparatus as our own. But now, we must, in all conscience, admit the contrary; the apparatus we call ours is, in fact, still quite alien to us; it is a bourgeois and tsarist hotch-potch and there has been no possibility of getting rid of it in the course of the past five years without the help of other countries and because we have been "busy" most of the time with military engagements and the fight against famine.

It is quite natural that in such circumstances the "freedom to secede from the union" by which we justify ourselves will be a mere scrap of paper, unable to defend the non-Russians from the onslaught of that really Russian man, the Great-Russian chauvinist, in substance a rascal and a tyrant, such as the typical Russian bureaucrat is. There is no doubt that the infinitesimal percentage of Soviet and sovietised workers will drown in that tide of chauvinistic Great-Russian riffraff like a fly in milk.

It is said in defense of this measure that the People's Commissariats directly concerned with national psychology and national education were set up as separate bodies. But there the question arises: can these People's Commissariats be made quite independent? and secondly: were we careful enough to take measures to provide the non-Russians with a real safeguard against the truly Russian bully? I do not think we took such measures although we could and should have done so.

I think that Stalin's haste and his infatuation with pure administration, together with his spite against the notorious "nationalist-socialism," played a fatal role here. In politics spite generally plays the basest of roles. . . .

Here we have an important question of principle: how is internationalism to be understood?[11]

Lenin

December 30, 1922
Taken down by M. V.

---

[11]After this, the following phrase was crossed out in the shorthand text: "It seems to me that our comrades have not studied this important question of principle sufficiently."

A Chronology of V. I. Lenin's Life
(1870–1924)

1870 *April*: V. I. Lenin (born Vladimir Illich Ulyanov) is born in 1870 in the town of Simbirsk on the Volga River

1887 *June*: Lenin graduates from gymnasium (high school)

1887 *May*: Lenin's brother Alexander is executed

1887 *August*: Lenin enters the University of Kazan

1887 *December*: Lenin is arrested for participating in student protests

1887 *December*: Lenin is expelled from the University and exiled to the village of Kokushkino near Kazan' for one year

1891 *November*: Lenin graduates from the University of St. Petersburg

1893 *Autumn*: Lenin joins a Marxist circle in St. Petersburg

1894 Nicholas II becomes tsar

1895 *December*: Lenin is arrested and spends 14 months in prison.

1897 *February*: Lenin is sentenced to three years exile in Eastern Siberia

1898 *July*: Lenin marries Nadezhda Konstantinovna Krupskaia

**1898–
1900** In exile, Lenin writes *The Development of Capitalism in Russia*

1900 *July*: On returning from exile, Lenin goes abroad to Switzerland and other countries

1901 Lenin, who has been known until this point as Ulyanov, adopts the name N. Lenin

**1901–
1902** Lenin writes *What Is to Be Done?* and edits *Iskra* (*The Spark*)

1903 *July–August*: Lenin attends the Second Congress of the Russian Social-Democratic Workers' Party and helps to split the party into factions: Bolsheviks and Mensheviks

1904 *February*: Beginning of Russo-Japanese War

1904   *December*: Surrender of Port Arthur to Japanese

1905   *January*: The "Bloody Sunday" massacre; The First Russian Revolution begins

1905   *June–July*: Lenin writes *Two Tactics of Social Democracy in the Democratic Revolution*

1905   *September*: Treaty of Portsmouth ending Russo-Japanese War is signed

1905   *October*: October Manifesto: Nicholas II promises a constitution and an elected representative assembly

1905   *November*: Lenin returns to Russia amidst the Revolution of 1905

1907   *November*: Lenin leaves Helsinki (then part of the Russian Empire) for Geneva and then Paris

1912   *January*: Lenin plays a leading role in the Sixth Party Conference in Prague, which is in effect a Bolshevik conference

1912   *April*: Lenin helps to found the legal Bolshevik newspaper *Pravda* (The Truth)

1914   *August*: World War I begins

1915   *September*: Lenin attends the First International Socialist Conference in Switzerland and demands a new revolutionary International

1917   *February (March)*: February Revolution; Nicholas II abdicates

1917   *April*: Lenin travels on a German train to Sweden

1917   *April*: Lenin arrives at the Finland Station in Petrograd from Russian Finland

1917   *April*: Lenin reads his "April Theses" to party members, and it is readied for publication in *Pravda*

1917   *July*: Lenin writes *State and Revolution*

1917   *July–November*: Lenin is accused of being a German agent and goes into hiding

1917   *November*: Lenin leads the Second All-Russian Congress of Soviets and is elected the head of the government (the Council of the People's Commissars)

1918   *March*: The capital of Russia is transferred to Moscow; Lenin comes to Moscow

1918   *November*: Germany signs the armistice ending World War I

1919   *March*: Lenin opens the First Congress of the Communist International

1919   *June*: Signing of the Treaty of Versailles

1920 *December*: Poland invades Ukraine

1921 *March*: Lenin leads the Tenth Congress of the Communist Party, which proclaims the New Economic Policy

1922 *April*: Stalin appointed general secretary of the Communist Party

1922 *April*: Treaty of Rapallo signed between Russia and Germany

1922 *May*: Lenin suffers his first stroke

1922 *December*: Lenin suffers a second major stroke and other strokes follow

1922 *December*: Lenin begins dictating his "Letter to the Congress," which is later described as his "testament"

1922 *February*: Lenin dictates his last notes

1923 *March*: Lenin dictates his letter to Stalin

1923 *March*: Lenin suffers a massive, incapacitating stroke

1924 *January*: Lenin dies

Questions for Consideration

1. What experiences informed Lenin's ideology and interest in revolution?
2. What kind of party did Lenin seek to create (Documents 2–3)? Why did he ban factions at the Tenth Party Congress (Documents 38–40)?
3. Describe Lenin's attitude toward different social classes and social groups.
4. To which social groups did Lenin appeal—first as a revolutionary and then later as a party leader?
5. How did Lenin regard his opponents outside and inside the party?
6. What were Lenin's stated objectives and what might have been his unstated objectives in adopting War Communism (Documents 15, 17, 28, 30, 33) and the New Economic Policy (Documents 42, 43, 44, 46)?
7. Was the Bolshevik political system consistent with the New Economic Policy or were there some contradictions?
8. How important was world revolution to Lenin?
9. To what extent can Leninism be described as an ideology separate from Marxism? To what extent can Leninism be described as a logical outgrowth of Marxism?
10. What were Lenin's long-term goals?
11. Describe Lenin's place in Russian and world history.
12. Provide a rationale for excluding some documents from Lenin's *Complete Works*. Why were the original versions of the documents published only after the fall of the USSR?
13. To what extent was Lenin an idealist, an ideological actor, or a pragmatist?

Selected Bibliography

V. I. LENIN'S WORKS AND DOCUMENTS

Buranov, Y., *Lenin's Will: Falsified and Forbidden. From the Secret Archives of the Former Soviet Union.* Amherst, N.Y.: Prometheus Books, 1994.

Lenin, V. I., *Collected Works.* 45 vols. Moscow: Progress Publishers, 1960–1970.

Lenin, V. I. *Lenin's Final Fight: Speeches and Writings 1922–23.* New York: Pathfinder, 1995.

Pipes, R., ed. *The Unknown Lenin: From the Secret Archive.* New Haven, Conn.: Yale University Press, 1996.

Tucker, R. C., ed. *The Lenin Anthology.* New York: Norton, 1975.

SECONDARY LITERATURE

Brovkin, V., ed. *The Bolsheviks in Russian Society.* New Haven, Conn.: Yale University Press, 1997.

Carrère d'Encausse, H. *Lenin.* New York: Holmes and Meier, 2001.

Clark, R. W. *Lenin.* New York: Harper and Row, 1988.

Conquest, R. *Lenin.* London: Viking, 1972.

Fitzpatrick, S., A. Rabinovich, and R. Stites, eds. *Russia in the Era of NEP.* Bloomington: Indiana University Press, 1991.

Haimson, L. *The Russian Marxists and the Origins of Bolshevism.* Cambridge, Mass.: Harvard University Press, 1955.

Harding, N. *Lenin's Political Thought.* 2 vols. New York: St. Martin's, 1977, 1981.

Koenker, D., W. Rosenberg, and R. Suny, eds. *Party, State, and Society in the Russian Civil War.* Bloomington: Indiana University Press, 1988.

Le Blanc, P. *Lenin and the Revolutionary Party.* Atlantic Highlands, N.J.: Humanities Press International, 1990.

Liebman, M. *Leninism under Lenin.* Atlantic Highlands, N.J.: Humanities Press International, 1985.

Lukács, G. *Lenin: A Study on the Unity of His Thought.* Cambridge, Mass.: MIT Press, 1971.

Marples, D. R. *Lenin's Revolution: Russia, 1917–1921.* Harlow, England: Longman, 2000.

Pomper, P. *Lenin, Trotsky, and Stalin: The Intelligentsia and Power*. New York: Columbia University Press, 1990.

Rice, C. *Lenin: Portrait of a Professional Revolutionary*. London: Cassell, 1990.

Schapiro, Leonard, and Peter Reddaway, eds., *Lenin. The Man, the Theorist, the Leader: A Reappraisal*. New York: F. A. Praeger, 1967.

Service, R. *Lenin: A Biography*. Cambridge, Mass.: Harvard University Press, 2000.

Service, R. *Lenin: A Political Life*. 3 vols. Bloomington: Indiana University Press, 1985, 1991, 1995.

Shub, David. *Lenin*. Garden City, N.Y.: Doubleday, 1948.

Treadgold, D. *Lenin and His Rivals: The Struggle for Russia's Future*. 1898–1906. New York: F. A. Praeger, 1955.

Tumarkin, N. *Lenin Lives*. Cambridge, Mass.: Harvard University Press, 1997.

Ulam, A. B. *Lenin and the Bolsheviks: The Intellectual and Political History of the Triumph of Communism in Russia*. London: Secker and Warburg, 1966.

Valentinov, N. *The Early Years of Lenin*. Ann Arbor: University of Michigan Press, 1969.

Volkogonov, Dmitri. *Lenin: A New Biography*. New York: Free Press, 1994.

Volkogonov, D. *Lenin: Life and Legacy*. London: HarperCollins, 1994.

Williams, B. *Lenin*. Harlow, England and New York: Longman, 2000.

Williams, R. C., *Lenin and His Critics, 1904–1914*. Bloomington: Indiana University Press, 1986.

Wolfe, B. D. *Three Who Made a Revolution: A Biographical History*. New York: Dell Publishing, 1964.

in, V. I. (*cont.*)
    ouse arrest of, 152
    mmediate Tasks of the Soviet
        Government, The," 94–97
    mpending Catastrophe and How to
        Combat It, The," 29, 57–58
    mperialism, the Highest Stage of
        Capitalism," 44–45
    terview Granted to an *Izvestia*
        Correspondent in Connection with the
        Left Socialist-Revolutionary Revolt,"
        69–71
    t active years of, 22–25
    t thoughts of, 156–61
    acy of, 1–31
    etter to American Workers," 86–88
    etter to A. V. Lunacharsky," 142–43
    etter to G. E. Zinoviev," 75
    etter to G. I. Blagonravov and V. D.
        Bonch-Bruevich," 73–74
    tter to I. V. Stalin," 139–41, 155–56
    tter to Maxim Gorky," 78–79
    tter to Stalin for Politburo of RCP(B)
        C," 151–52
    tter to the Congress: Continuation of
        e Notes," 152–55, 164
    tter to the Workers and Peasants
        ropos of the Victory over Kolchak,"
        –86
    ter to V. M. Molotov for the
        embers of the CC of RCP(B),"
        5–49
    ter to V. M. Molotov for the Politburo
        the CC of RCP(B)," 143–44
    opolization of power during Civil War
        , 61–102
    ctive in New Economic Policy,
        5–29
    Co-operation," 157–59
    of the Fundamental Questions of
        Revolution," 59–60
    n Letter to the Delegates of the All-
        ssian Congress of Peasants'
        puties, An," 53–56
    nization of Food Detachments,"
        –98
    y Crises, The," 104
    y Organization and Party Literature,
        e," 42–44
    state, as creator of, 17–20
    cal Report of the Central
        mmittee of the RCP(B) to the
        nenth Congress of the RCP(B),"
        –29
    cal Report of the Central
        mmittee to the Eighth All-Russian
        ference of the RCP(B)," 101–2
    cal Report to the Ninth All-Russian
        ference of the RCP(B)," 92–93
    l testament, 26

"Preliminary Draft Resolution of the
    Tenth Congress of the RCP on Party
    Unity," 108–11
"Question of Nationalities or
    'Autonomization,' The," 159–61
removal from power, 150–61
"Report of the Council of People's
    Commissars on the Fifth All-Russian
    Congress of Soviets," 76–77
"Report on the International Situation
    and the Fundamental Tasks of the
    Communist International to the
    Second Congress of Comintern,"
    90–92
"Report on the Political Work of the
    Central Committee of the RCP(B) on
    Tenth Congress of the RCP(B),"
    112–14
"Report on the Substitution of a Tax in
    Kind for the Surplus Grain
    Appropriation System," 115–19
"Resolution on the National Question,"
    29, 52–53
"Resolution on War and Peace," 82–83
as revolutionary, 7–12
"Rough Draft of Theses Concerning the
    Peasants," 114–15
"Socialist Fatherland Is in Danger!, The,"
    80–81
"Speech at the Opening Session of the
    Congress," 88–89
"Speech in Favor of the Resolution on the
    War," 51–52
"Speech to Propagandists on Their Way
    to the Provinces," 67–69
"Speech to the First All-Russian Congress
    of Land Departments, Poor Peasants'
    Committees, and Communes,"
    99–100
State and Revolution, The, 16, 45–48, 142,
    163
strokes, 26, 131*n*, 164
struggle for power, 37–60
"Summary of Lenin's Remarks at the
    Conference Lessons of October," 25
"Summary of Lenin's Remarks at the
    Conference of the Delegates to the
    Tenth Congress of the RCP(B)—
    Supporters of the Platform of Ten,"
    106–8
"Tasks of the Proletariat in the Present
    Revolution (April Theses), The," 49–51
"Telegram to All Provincial and Regional
    Party Committees of the RCP(B),"
    123–25
"Telegram to the Penza Gubernia
    Executive Committee of the Soviets,"
    77–78
"Telegram to V. L. Paniushkin," 74
theorist of revolution, 37–48

Index

agricultural policy, 7, 54, 99, 134. *See also*
    food; grain; peasants
Alexander (Lenin's brother), 5*f*, 7, 162
Alexander II, tsar, 3–4, 7
Alexander III, tsar, 7
Allies, 20, 76, 83–84
All-Russian Central Executive Committee,
    62*n*, 65, 70*n*, 71*n*, 97, 122, 136
All-Russian Communist Party, 18
All-Russian Congress of Producers, 107
All-Russian Congress of Soviets of Workers'
    and Soldiers' Deputies, 17, 62, 62*n*, 63,
    66*n*, 163
All-Russian Extraordinary Commission for
    Struggle against Counterrevolution,
    Sabotage, and Speculation, 69, 73, 77,
    139
All-Russian Party Conference, Ninth, 92
All-Ukrainian Party Conference, 109*n*
American Relief Administration (ARA),
    134
anti-Bolshevik popular uprisings and shift in
    policy, 111–15
"April Theses," 14, 37, 49, 163
Armand, Inessa, 150, 150*n*
Armenia, 20, 52
arrests, mass, 74
Asia. *See* Central Asia
Austria-Hungary, 49
autonomization, 159–60
Avksentyev, Nikolai Dmitrievich, 66, 66*n*
Azerbaijan, 20

Baltic region, 20, 80
Berlin agreement, 136, 138
Bismarck, Otto von, 7
Black Hundred clergy, 147
black market, 21
Black Sea, control of straits of, 51
Blagonravov, Grigorii Ivanovich, 73–74, 74*n*
"Bloody Sunday" massacre, 163

Blumkin, Yakov, 70*n*
Boer War, 19
Bolsheviks. *See also* Communist Party;
    Russian Communist Party
    agricultural program of, 54
    Central Committee, 18, 26, 63–64, 101–2,
        125–29, 153–55
    challenges of, 67
    Constituent Assembly, promise to
        convene, 65
    "Decree on the Press" and, 141–42
    disputes and opposition in (1920–1921),
        104–6
    economic policy and, 94, 103
    as the majority, 10
    as members of All-Russian Central
        Executive Committee, 62*n*
    as party of order, 57–58
    rule and the new soviet state, 17–20
    Russian Orthodox Christianity and,
        146–47
    seizure of power by, 37–60
    split with Mensheviks, 39, 162
    support for, 54
    terror against Mensheviks and Socialist-
        Revolutionaries, 135–36
    treaties with Britain and France and,
        51
    uprisings against, 111–15
Bolshoi Theatre, 143–44
Bonch-Bruevich, Vladimir Dmitrievich,
    73–74
bourgeoisie. *See also* capitalism
    elimination of, 135
    ethics of, 145
    struggle against proletariat, 137
    truce with, 94–95
"bourgeois intelligentsia," 78–79
Britain. *See* Great Britain
British Labor Party, 93*n*
Bukharin, N. I., 25, 80, 138, 152, 154

Bulgaria, 49
Buranov, Yuri, 152
Byelorussians, 52, 80, 159

Cadet Party, 51, 64, 66, 79, 139
camps, forced-labor and concentration, 73
capitalism. *See also* bourgeoisie
  appeals to overthrow, 86–88
  domination of monopolist associations of
    big employers, 44–45, 47
  halt to offensive against, 94–97
  peasant, 125–26
  Russian, 126
  state, 94, 125–28, 131, 133
Central Asia, 20, 112
Central Committee of the Trade Union of
  Transport Workers, 105, 105*n*
Central Executive Committee of the
  Soviets, 17, 62, 66, 144*n*
Cheka. *See* All-Russian Extraordinary
  Commission for Struggle against
  Counterrevolution, Sabotage, and
  Speculation
Chernov, V. M., 66, 66*n*
Chernyshevsky, Nicholai, 39
Chicherin, G. V., 24
Civil War, 20, 57–58, 86
  Bolshevik forces in, 146
  economic strategy and, 101, 103
  end of, 130
  internal crisis after, 132
  monopolization of power during,
    61–102
  role of peasants in, 133
  victory in, 52, 112
  War Communism and, 97
"class enemy," 19, 30, 67, 73–74
class struggle, 46, 53
CLD. *See* Council of Labor and Defense
Collected Works (Lenin), 2
collective farms, 99–100
colonial peoples, revolutionary potential of,
  90–92
Comintern. *See* Communist International
  (Comintern)
command economy, 61, 94–102
Committee of Action, 93*n*
Committee of the Members of the
  Constituent Assembly (Komuch),
  114*n*
Communist International (Comintern), 24,
  88–91, 129–34, 136–38, 163
Communist Party, 90–92, 118, 144. *See
  also* Bolsheviks; Russian Communist
  Party; Russian Social-Democratic
  Workers' Party
Constituent Assembly, 17, 65–67
Constitutional Democratic Party, 17
co-operatives, 120, 121, 157–59
Council of Action in England, 93

Council of Labor and Defense (CLD), 121,
  122
Council of People's Commissars (CPC), 16,
  81, 122*n*
  decree abolishing private trade, 99
  decree forbidding sale of grain, 21
  decree for disposal of material resources,
    121
  decree instituting food requisition,
    97–98
  Lenin's election to, 163
  preservation of Bolshoi Opera and Ballet
    and, 143–44
Council of Workers' and Peasants' Defense,
  122*n*
cultural system, 141–49
Czechoslovak mutiny, 23

death penalty, 22
"Declaration of Rights of the Working and
  Exploited People, The," 66
"Decree on the Arrest of the Leaders of
  the Civil War against the Revolution,"
  64
"Decree on the Press," 142
democracy, 48, 53
"democratic centralism," 90
Democratic Centralists, 103–4, 107,
  109–10
Denikin, Anton Ivanovich, 83, 83*n*, 85, 102,
  113
Development of Capitalism in Russia, The, 9,
  162
dictatorship
  counterrevolutionary, 56
  one-party, 64
Discussion Bulletin (*Diskussionny Listok*),
  110*n*
Don Cossaks, 19, 63*n*
Don region, peasant rebellion in, 112
Dostoevsky, F., 23
draft, military, 4
"Draft Decree on the Dissolution of the
  Constituent Assembly," 65–67
"Draft Resolution on the Question of the
  New Economic Policy for the Xth
  Conference of the RCP(B)," 119
Dzerzhinsky, F. E., 69, 71

Economist, 140*n*, 141
economy, 61, 94–102, 129–35
Engels, Friedrich, 7, 37, 46, 48
Estonia, independence of, 20, 51
Europe, 2, 89
executions, 74

factionalism, 109
famine, 76, 77, 94, 123, 134, 146
farms, collective, 99–100
February Revolution of 1917, 28, 48, 163

Ferster, O., 151–52, 151*n*
Finland, independence of, 20, 52, 80
"Five Years of the Russian Revolution and
  the Prospects of the World Revolution:
  Report to the Fourth Congress of the
  Communist International," 129–34
food. *See also* agricultural policy; grain;
  peasants
  maintaining supply, 67, 97, 123–24
  requisition (*podrazverstka*), 97–98,
    101–2
France
  Civil War and, 20
  Czechoslovak mutiny and, 76
  Provisional Government's loyalty to,
    49
  support for anti-Bolshevik rebellion by,
    83–84
  treaty with, 51–52
Futurists, 142–43, 142*n*

German Social Democratic Party (SPD), 7
Germany
  assassination of ambassador to Soviet
    Russia, 69
  Lenin's position on, 80–81
  making politics in, 92–93
  paying Bolsheviks to hinder war effort,
    56
  peace with, 82–83
  Soviet republics in Bavaria, 89
  support of the Whites by, 84
  Ukraine, attempts to control, 20
  World War I and, 49
glavki (*glavnyie upravleniia*), 108*n*
Gorka, Krasnaya, 79
Gorky, Maxim, 78–79, 134–35, 134*n*
grain, 21, 61, 85, 97, 115–17. *See also*
  agricultural policy; food; peasants
Great Britain,
  Czechoslovak mutiny and, 76
  Provisional Government's loyalty to, 49
  support for anti-Bolshevik rebellion by,
    83–84
  trade agreement with, 24
  treaty with, 51
Great Reforms, 3–4
Gregorian calendar, 31*n*
gubernias, 120, 147*n*

Ilin, 9. *See also* Lenin, V. I.
"Immediate Tasks of the Soviet
  Government, The," 94–97
*Impending Catastrophe and How to Combat
  It, The*, 29, 57–58
imperialism, international, 93
*Imperialism, the Highest Stage of
  Capitalism*, 44–45
Internationals. *See* Communist International
  (Comintern)

"Interview Granted to an [...]
  Correspondent in C[...]
  Left Socialist-Revolu[...]
  69–71
Iskra (The Spark), 10, 3[...]

Japan, 10, 20, 84
Julian calendar, 31*n*

Kalinin, M., 146–48
Kamenev, L. B., 25, 14[...]
Kerensky, A., 66, 86
  appointment as pres[...]
  as imperialist robbe[...]
  resistance to Bolshe[...]
Klemperer, G., 151, 1[...]
Kolchak, A. V., 83–86[...]
Korolenko, V. G., 79, [...]
Kozlovsky, A. N., 113[...]
Krasnov, P. N., 63, 63[...]
Kronstadt naval base[...]
  uprising at, 21, 1[...]
Krupskaia, N. K., 8–[...]
kulaks, 20, 67–68
  equalization of, 11[...]
  grain requisition f[...]
  land reform for b[...]
  risings, 76, 76*n*[...]
  suppression of, 7[...]

land, promised to p[...]
Latvia, independen[...]
Left Socialist-Revol[...]
"'Left-Wing' Comm[...]
  Disorder," 89-[...]
Lena goldfields, 1[...]
Lenin, V. I.
  Bolshevik seizu[...]
  chronology of l[...]
  decline of, 25–[...]
  "Decree on the[...]
    the Civil Wa[...]
    64
  development [...]
    22–25, 103-[...]
  "Draft Decree[...]
    Constituent[...]
  "Draft Resolu[...]
    New Econo[...]
    Conference[...]
  family of, 3, 5[...]
  "Five Years [...]
    and the Pr[...]
    Revolution[...]
    Congress[...]
    Internatio[...]
  foreign poli[...]
  founding of [...]
  Germany, [...]
  health of, 1[...]

Le[...]
  h[...]
"[...]
"[...]
"[...]
"[...]
la[...]
la[...]
le[...]
"L[...]
"L[...]
"L[...]
L[...]
"L[...]
"L[...]
"L[...]
  C
"L[...]
"L[...]
"L[...]
  M
"L[...]
  1[...]
"L[...]
  o[...]
mo[...]
by[...]
obj[...]
  1[...]
"O[...]
"O[...]
  th[...]
"O[...]
  R[...]
  D[...]
"O[...]
  9[...]
"P[...]
"P[...]
Th[...]
party[...]
"Poli[...]
  Co[...]
  Ele[...]
  125[...]
"Poli[...]
  Co[...]
  Co[...]
"Poli[...]
  Co[...]
politi[...]

threats to the revolution and, 103–51
"To Workers, Soldiers, and Peasants!,"
  62
"Urgent Tasks of Our Movement, The,"
  38
"We Have Paid Too Much," 135–38
What Is to Be Done? 10, 16, 37, 39–42,
  162
youth of, 3–7
"Letter to American Workers," 86–88
"Letter to A. V. Lunacharsky," 142–43
"Letter to G. E. Zinoviev," 75
"Letter to G. I. Blagonravov and
  V. D. Bonch-Bruevich," 73–74
"Letter to I. V. Stalin," 139–41, 155–56
"Letter to Maxim Gorky," 78–79
"Letter to Stalin for Politburo of RCP(B)
  CC," 151–52
"Letter to the Congress: Continuation of the
  Notes," 152–55, 164
"Letter to the Workers and Peasants
  apropos of the Victory over Kolchak,"
  83–86
"Letter to V. M. Molotov for the Members
  of the CC of RCP(B)," 145–49
"Letter to V. M. Molotov for the Politburo
  of the CC of RCP(B)," 143–44
Lezhnev, I. G., 139, 141, 141n
Lithuania, independence of, 20, 52
Lunacharsky, A. V., 143n, 144

Marx, Karl, 7, 37, 46
Marxism
  capitalism and, 102, 118
  educated youth and, 40
  Lenin's fidelity to, 7, 30, 92
  notion of synthesis of opposites, 3
  as opposite of populism, 8
  state capitalism and, 127
Mayakovsky, Vladimir, 142–43, 143n
Mensheviks, 10. *See also* Russian Social-
    Democratic Workers' Party
  Bolshevik coalition with, 63
  deportation of, 139–40
  Kolchak movement and, 86
  Komuch and, 114
  loss of influence, 69
  as majority at First All-Russian Congress
    of Soviets, 62n
  resistance of, 95
  split with Bolsheviks, 39, 57, 162
  terror against, 135–36
Military Revolutionary Committee of the
  Petrograd Soviet, 14
Ministry of Foreign Affairs of the
  Provisional Government, 24
Mirbach, Count Whilhelm von, 69, 70
Molotov, V. M., 123–25, 143–44, 146–49,
  147n
Moslem population, 52

mummification of Lenin, 2
Mysl' (Thought), 141, 141n

New Economic Policy (NEP), 22, 30, 164
  anti-Bolshevik popular uprisings,
    111–15
  co-operatives and, 157–58
  development of, 103–51
  Lenin's objective in, 115–29
  newspapers. *See* press, the
Nicholas II, 40n, 42, 162, 163

oblasts, 120
October Manifesto, 163
October Revolution, 14, 114, 154
  anti-Bolshevik revolts and, 83
  as beginning of socialist revolution, 66
  democracy and, 28
"On Co-operation," 157–59
"One of the Fundamental Questions of the
  Revolution," 59–60
one-party system, institutionalization of,
  135–41
"On Party Unity," 106
"Open Letter to the Delegates of the All-
  Russian Congress of Peasants'
  Deputies, An," 53–56
Organizational Bureau (Orgburo), 18, 25
"Organization of Food Detachments,"
  97–98
Orgburo (Organizational Bureau), 18, 25

parliamentary system, 46, 66
"Party Crises, The," 104
Party of Left Socialist-Revolutionaries (Left
  SRs), 65
"Party Organization and Party Literature,
  The," 42–44
peasant capitalism, 125–26
peasant communes, 6
peasants. *See also* agricultural policy; food;
    grain
  demands of the state on, 85
  land and, 53–54, 94
  management of relations with, 130
  New Economic Policy and, 132–33
  Poor Peasants' Committees, 99–100
  rebellions of, 103, 112
  relationship with working class, 116
  reluctance to sell surpluses, 97
  suppression of, 77
  transfer of power to, 59–60
  war against, 67–68
Penza Soviet of Deputies, 97–98
People's Commissariat for Food Supply, 98,
  101, 121
People's Commissariat of Foreign Affairs,
  16, 24
Peshkov, A. N. *See* Gorky, Maxim
"Platform of the Ten, The," 104–6, 107

Poland, 20, 52, 92–93, 150, 164
Politburo, 18, 25, 136
"Political Report of the Central Committee
of the RCP(B) to the Eleventh
Congress of the RCP(B)," 125–29
"Political Report of the Central Committee
to the Eighth All-Russian Conference
of the RCP(B)," 101–2
"Political Report to the Ninth All-Russian
Conference of the RCP(B)," 92–93
"Political Situation, The," 56–57
Poor Peasants' Committees, 99–100
Popular Socialists (*Naridnyie Sotsialisty*),
139, 139*n*
populists, 6, 8
Portsmouth, Treaty of, 163
Pravda (The Truth), 23, 163
"Preliminary Draft Resolution of the Tenth
Congress of the RCP on Party Unity,"
108–11
press, the, 42–43, 141–42
private ownership, 125, 130
proletariat, 59–60, 130, 137
Provisional Government, 48–50, 54, 56, 62
Provisional Workers' and Peasants'
Government, 72
Pyatakov, I. L., 153, 154, 154*n*

"Question of Nationalities or
'Autonomization,' The," 159–61

Radek, K. B., 138, 138*n*
red, 19
Red Army, 84–85, 92, 97, 113, 114*n*
Red Guards, 65, 81
"red terror," 78
religion, 145–46
"Report of the Council of People's
Commissars on the Fifth All-Russian
Congress of Soviets," 76–77
"Report on the International Situation and
the Fundamental Tasks of the
Communist International to the Second
Congress of Comintern," 90–92
"Report on the Political Work of the
Central Committee of the RCP(B) on
Tenth Congress of the RCP(B),"
112–14
"Report on the Substitution of a Tax in
Kind for the Surplus Grain
Appropriation System," 115–19
requisitioning, 21, 101–2, 134
"Resolution of the Central Committee of the
RSDLP(B) on the Opposition within
the Central Committee," 63–64
"Resolution on the National Question," 29,
52–53
"Resolution on War and Peace," 82–83
revolution, 38–48, 56–57, 88–89, 103–51
"revolutionary defencism," 51
revolutionary practice, 39–42

Revolutionary Tribunals, 124
Revolution of 1905, 10, 37, 163
Right Socialist-Revolutionaries, 66, 95
"robber tax," 134
"Role and Tasks of the Trade Unions, The,"
103
"Rough Draft of Theses Concerning the
Peasants," 114–15
Russia
capitalism and, 126
class hierarchy in, 4
as democratic republic, 55
economic challenges of prerevolutionary,
4–7
famine in, 134
foreign intervention in, 83
Imperial, 31
independence of, 159
of Lenin's youth, 3–7
secret treaties with Britain and France,
51
Russian Communist Party, 112–14, 123–29,
143–44, 146–49, 151–52. *See also*
Communist Party; Russian Social-
Democratic Workers' Party
Eighth Congress, 18, 20, 103
Eleventh Congress, 18, 22, 125
Ninth Congress, 20, 21
Seventh Congress, 18, 19
Tenth Congress, 21, 22, 30, 104, 116,
164
Thirteenth Congress, 152
Russian Orthodox Christianity, 146–47
Russian Poland, Treaty of Brest-Litovsk
and, 80
Russian Social-Democratic Workers' Party.
See also Bolsheviks; Mensheviks
banning of political activity of, 136
importance of theory in, 39–40
split into factions, 162
trade unions and, 41–42
Russo-Japanese War, 19, 162

Samara, 7, 114*n*
secede, right of nations to, 52–53
Second International Working Men's
Association, 49*n*
serfdom, 3–4
show trial, 136
Shuya, clash between Bolseviks and church
activists, 146–47
Siberia,
exile in, 37
Japanese interest in, 20
liberation of, 84–85
peasant rebellion in Western, 112
Social-Democratic Workers' Party. *See*
Russian Social-Democratic Workers'
Party
socialism
Russia proceeding toward, 130

theory of, 41
transition to, 96
"Socialist Fatherland Is in Danger!, The,"
    80–81
Socialist-Revolutionary Party (SRs)
    agricultural program of, 54
    Bolshevik coalition with, 62n, 63
    Constituent Assembly and, 17, 66
    death penalty for members, 137
    Komuch and, 114n
    Kronstadt events and, 113
    as majority of First All-Russian Congress
        of Soviets, 62n
    revolution betrayed by, 57–58
    support for Bolsheviks, 65
    support for Kolchak movement, 86
    terror against, 135–36
    trial of leaders of, 22
soviet power, 17, 62
Soviet Russia, constitution of, 66n
Soviets of Agricultural Laborers' Deputies,
    50
Soviets of Workers', Soldiers' and Peasants'
    Deputies, 50, 65
Soviet state
    Bolshevik rule and the new, 17–20
    Lenin and founding of, 1–3
Spark, The. See Iskra
SPD. See German Social Democratic Party
"Speech at the Opening Session of the
    Congress," 88–89
"Speech in Favor of the Resolution on the
    War," 51–52
"Speech to Propagandists on Their Way to
    the Provinces," 67–69
"Speech to the First All-Russian Congress
    of Land Departments, Poor Peasants'
    Committees, and Communes,"
    99–100
spiritual system, toward a single, 141–49
"spontaneous element," 40–41
SRs. See Socialist-Revolutionary Party (SRs)
Stalin, I. V., 27f, 29f
    appointed general secretary, 164
    authority of, 151, 153–54
    efforts to reduce the autonomy of the
        nationalities, 26
    Lenin's challenges to, 159
    Lenin's wish to remove from power,
        155
    removal of Lenin from power, 150–52
State and Revolution, The, 16, 45–48, 142,
    163
"state capitalism," 94, 125–28, 131, 133
St. Petersburg, industrial war of 1896, 40
strikes, 41, 103
"Summary of Lenin's Remarks at the
    Conference of the Delegates to the
    Tenth Congress of the RCP(B)—
    Supporters of the Platform of Ten,"
    106–8

Supreme Council of the National Economy,
    108n
syndicalism (trade unionism), 104–6

"Tasks of the Proletariat in the Present
    Revolution (April Theses), The,"
    49–51
"Tasks of the Youth Leagues, The,"
    144–45
taxes, 118, 134
"Telegram to All Provincial and Regional
    Party Committees of the RCP(B),"
    123–25
"Telegram to the Penza Gubernia Executive
    Committee of the Soviets," 77–78
"Telegram to V. L. Paniushkin," 74
Temporary Revolutionary Committee, 112
terrorism, 8, 70, 75, 82, 83
"To Workers, Soldiers, and Peasants!" 62
trade, 99, 123
Trade Unionism, 41
trade unions, 22
    British, 93n
    leaders of, 87n
    "Platform of the Ten, The," 103–8
    role in party organization, 39
    struggles of, 41
Trans-Caucasia, 159
Treaty of Brest-Litovsk, 80
Treaty of Rapallo, 24, 164
Treaty of Versailles, 92–93, 163
Trotsky, L. D.
    centrist position of, 153–54, 154n
    excluded from conflict with church,
        147–48
    excluded from new government, 63
    as follower of Lenin, 156
    head of People's Commissariat of Foreign
        Affairs, 16
    labor armies and, 101
    Lenin's "Letter to the Congress" and,
        153
    as successor of Lenin, 25
    suggestion for forced requisitioning, 21
    support for revolutionary war, 80
    trade unions and, 103–4
    wish to resign, 108
    Two Tactics of Social Democracy in the
        Democratic Revolution, 163
Turkey, 49, 51

Ukraine
    famine in, 134
    German attempts to control, 20, 81
    independence of, 52, 159
    peasant rebellion in, 112
    Poland invades, 164
    Treaty of Brest-Litovsk and, 80
Ulianova, M. I., 152
Ulyanov, V. I. See Lenin, V. I.
Union of the Soviet Republics (USSR), 159

United States, 83–84, 134
Universal Military Service Statute of
     1874, 4
Urals area, 84–85, 114*n*, 134
"Urgent Tasks of Our Movement, The,"
     38

VChK. *See* All-Russian Extraordinary
     Commission for Struggle against
     Counterrevolution, Sabotage, and
     Speculation
Volga region, 112, 114*n*, 134

War, the Fatherland, and Mankind, 79
War Communism
     dangers of, 114–15
     failure of, 150
     as ideology or pragmatism, 20–22
     invention of command economy and,
        94–102
     law of, 129
     loss of support for, 112
     political situation resulting from, 103
     private trade, 99
     state monopoly over food supply, 61
"We Have Paid Too Much," 135–38
What Is to Be Done? 10, 16, 37, 39–42,
     162

white guards, 108, 111, 113–14, 133
Workers' Opposition, 22, 103–4, 107,
     109–10, 128
working class
     control of factories by, 94
     New Economic Policy and, 132
     political development of, 38
     power in hands of, 159
     relationship with peasants, 116
     role in party organization, 39
     transfer of power to, 59–60
     uprisings in South Africa, 137*n*
Working People's Socialist Party, 139*n*
world revolution, 79–93
World War I, 19, 37, 53, 79–93, 163

Young Communist League, 144
Yudenich, N. N., 83, 83*n*, 113
Zinoviev, G. E., 130, 156
     letter to, 75
     October Revolution and, 154
     questions Lenin's decision to seize power,
        25
     removal of Lenin from power and,
        150–51
     resolution on terror and, 82
     rivalry with Chicherin, 24
     trade unions and, 103